Seeking
Authenticity

Seeking
Authenticity

Essays

Walter Cummins

Del Sol Press
Washington, D.C.

Seeking Authenticity
by Walter Cummins

Published by Del Sol Press
Washington, D.C.

First printing 2022

Cover: Peter Selgin

Printed in the United States of America

ISBN 978-1-7344900-3-9

Thanks to Renée Ashley and William Eaton for their assistance in preparing this collection and to Peter Selgin for the cover design.

For Alison

Yet, grief is also the price of love, of caring so much for another person that her removal from my life becomes a source of great emotional pain. As much as the loss hurts, it's worth it for the richness her presence brought over many years.

Acknowledgments

These essays were first published in the following magazines:

Zeteo Journal
"Mechanical Production," "Photographing the Soul," "Bongo, Bongo, Bongo: The Other as Cartoon and Caricature," "Outliving Society's Capacity to Care," "The Sources of Morality," "Eating Intelligent Beings," "Seeking Cultural Diversity," "The Groups We Belong To," "Where Do Humans End?," "Real Dolls and Other Humanoids," "Will Robots Displace Humans?" "Downton Abbey and the End of a Way of Life," "Hard Times: Teaching Facts" "Guns, Death, Terrorism, The United States"

The Ekphrastic Review
"Seeing and Believing"

The Literary Review
"Bird in Words"

The Doctor TJ Eckelburg Review
"A Bendel Bonnet, A Shakespeare Sonnet," "Fear of Heights," ""Needles' Eyes, Wealth, Learning, and Virtue," What is College For?"

The Wrath-Bearing Tree
"Knowing Your Father: DNA and Identity."

Contents

Which reproduction of Rembrandt's "Old Man with a Golden Chain" comes closest to capturing the real painting? Have the three centuries since it sat on Rembrandt's easel altered the tones of the oils so that the original no longer exists? Will I ever be able to know the authentic work of art?

The essays in this collection were first published at various points over a decade or more. Each was written separately with an individual focus. But when I gathered them and reread, I discovered they were united by a common theme and that, unaware, I've been addressing variations of the question of authenticity.

What is the authentic way of seeing a painting, listening to music, getting a college education, grieving, working, recognizing animal rights, and more? These essays consider the possibilities, without answering the questions. I hope that's enough for them to be interesting.

Walter Cummins

Mechanical Reproduction

Distraction and concentration form polar opposites which may be stated as follows: A man who concentrates before a work of art is absorbed by it.... In contrast, the distracted mass absorbs the work of art. — Walter Benjamin, as translated by Harry Zohn

THE OTHER DAY WHEN I ASKED ALEXA on an Amazon Echo to play John Coltrane's "Wise One" and, a split second later, when McCoy Tyner's piano chords filled the room, two references came to mind—Walter Benjamin's 1935 essay on the work of art in the age of mechanical reproduction ("Das Kunstwerk im Zeitalter seiner technischen Reproduzierbarkeit") and a 1999 TV commercial for Quest broadband services now tagged on YouTube as "Every Movie." In that thirty-second scene, a bedraggled traveler appears in the front office of Roy's Motel, seemingly in the middle of nowhere. When he asks about in-room entertainment, the bored young woman behind the counter looks up from her book and says, "We've got every movie ever made in every language, day and night."

What would Walter Benjamin say about such phenomena more than eighty-five years after he wrote his essay? In 1999, the every-movie concept sounded like a futuristic fantasy. Today I can access, if not every, millions of songs and pieces of music with a spoken request to a round black disk. And via wi-fi, my iPad or iPhone can bring up, if not every, thousands of movies and TV shows in many languages. Quest, by the way, no longer exists. After steep financial losses, it merged with a company called Century Link in 2011. Quest is gone and forgotten. Meanwhile, more and more reproduced music and video are added to cyberspace every hour, including obsolete TV commercials.

In contrast, Benjamin's then-modern examples of mechanical reproduction were movies, photographs, and photograph recordings. His brief historical overview of techniques to reproduce art started with founding and stamping for objects such as bronzes and coins, followed by woodblocks for graphic art, and then print and lithography. Nothing immediately accessible at the press of a key or a voice command. No instant gratification in 1935. Now we live in an age of digital immediacy.

At the heart of the reproduction problem for Benjamin is loss of the art object's authenticity. He writes (in Harry Zohn's translation):

> One might generalize by saying: the technique of reproduction detaches the reproduced object from the domain of tradition. By making many reproductions it substitutes a plurality of copies for a unique existence. And in permitting the reproduction to meet the beholder or listener in his own particular situation, it reactivates the object reproduced. These two processes lead to a tremendous shattering of tradition which is the obverse of the contemporary crisis and renewal of mankind.[1]

The tradition shattered in the 1930s was shattered by the mass movements of Nazism and Soviet Communism, leading to "the liquidation of the traditional value of the cultural heritage." He singles out film as the "most powerful agent" of this destructiveness, probably because it was the most prevalent form of mass art at the time of his essay.

A generation of American intellectuals was profoundly influenced by what Benjamin—and John Berger, Susan Sontag, et al., after him—had to say about art in the age of mechanical reproduction. Berger, for example, argued that modern reproduction destroyed the aesthetic, cultural, and political authority of art. Because images "have become ephemeral, ubiquitous, insubstantial, available, valueless, free," they lack the aura of the original work of art.

Donald Trump may be considered the epitome of a society that values distraction over substance.

At stake for Benjamin, beyond the loss of artistic authority, is the role of reproduced art in the social and political destruction of his time. In his pre-World War II linking of politics and the manipulation of reproduced art, Benjamin concludes his essay by lamenting that the aesthetics of war supply "the artistic gratification of a sense perception that has been changed by technology." In his pessimism, he argues that mankind's "self-alienation has reached such a degree that it can experience its own destruction as an aesthetic pleasure of the first order."

I'd like to think that today's simulations of violent computer games, dystopian fiction, and apocalyptic videos satisfy the masses' inclinations to be entertained by the glamorous thrill of warfare. And thus, for the great majority, there's no entertainment value in, say, the news footage of bombings and chemical warfare in Syria.

While not violent, current political movements in much of the world glorify another form of destructiveness. Eight decades after Benjamin we face mass movements—arising both from the spontaneous anger of the disaffected and from their manipulations by some with authoritarian agendas of power and greed—that threaten the tradition of liberal democracy and the related notions of truth and social justice. Any information, no matter how authenticated, that conflicts with the delusions and goals of those in power is dismissed as "fake" news.

Of course, those in power have always tried to control news and information, and gullibility to propaganda seems a fact of human nature. What's different in the twentieth-first century is the exponential growth in the scale of disrupted and corrupted information because of the massive reproduction made possible by digital outlets. Thus, for example, the Russian hacking of the 2016 U.S. election and Cambridge Analytica stealing the Facebook data of millions. Never before have people publicly exposed so much of their personal lives in their seduction by the instant gratifications of digital reproduction, and never before have forces that wish to control them been able to undermine their beliefs and choices so easily.

Benjamin claims that there is a fundamental distinction between the times before and after mechanical reproduction. Before, he argues, art realized its "authentic" value through association with ritual, whether magic, spiritual, or secular (as in the art for art's sake cult of "beauty"). Mechanical reproduction, however, divorces art from ritual and moves it to the sphere of politics, a sphere Benjamin finds threatening: "But the instant the criterion of authenticity ceases to be applicable to artistic production, the total function of art is reversed. Instead of being based on ritual, it begins to be based on another practice—politics."

What lies behind this differentiation of ritual and politics and, by implication, of the authentic and the inauthentic? How could a work like Beethoven's Eroica symphony, which was dedicated to Napoleon, not be political and still be an authentic work of art? One could argue that all artistic messages have socio-political overtones, as a magnificent cathedral goes beyond architectural beauty by supporting a set of religious beliefs. Benjamin, however, would consider the cathedral, as a unique, ritual-based work of art, much more worthy and more authentic than the then-current movies he attacks in his essay. And perhaps the politics of Beethoven's symphony can be skipped over on the grounds that he was more interested in the aesthetic integrity of the work than in winning favor with a powerful leader or manipulating the masses? Or because of the work's artistic complexity, which demands engagement and commitment from the listener?

It seems Benjamin is conflating the political with the commercial; for him the problem is art produced primarily to appeal to and be bought by a mass audience though the marketing of its many reproductions. Such art must be easy to grasp. "The mass is a matrix from which all traditional behavior toward works of art issues today in a new form. Quantity has been transmuted into quality. The greatly increased mass of participants has produced a change in the mode of participation."[2]

The simplified appeal to a wide audience allows for political manipulation because the participation of the audience in such art is radically different from that called for by "authentic" art. While the Beethoven symphony demands concentration, reproduced art offers distraction. "Distraction and concentration form polar opposites . . . A man who concentrates before a work of art is absorbed by it. . . . In contrast, the distracted mass absorbs the work of art."

Benjamin's argument in his essay also leads me to think of the critic Dwight MacDonald and his essay, "A Theory of Mass Culture," written in 1953, almost two decades after Benjamin. MacDonald makes distinctions between High Culture, Mass Culture, and Middlebrow Culture.

High Culture would be typified by a Beethoven symphony. Mass culture, in contrast, he writes, "is imposed from above. It is fabricated by technicians hired by business; its audiences are passive consumers, their participation limited to the choice between buying and not buying. The Lords of Kitsch, in short, exploit the cultural needs of the masses in order to make a profit and/or to maintain their class rule—in Communist countries, only the second purpose obtains." His passive consumers are the distracted mass. Middlebrow Culture waters down the High with a touch of the Mass: "There is nothing more vulgar than sophisticated kitsch."

Although McDonald does not mention the Benjamin essay, he attributes the rise of Mass Culture to the technology behind mechanical reproduction: "Business enterprise found a profitable market in the cultural demands of the newly awakened [since the early 1800s] masses, and the advance of technology made possible the cheap production of books, periodicals, pictures, music, and furniture, in sufficient quantities to satisfy this market. Modern technology also created new media such as the movies and television which are specially well adapted to mass manufacture and distribution."

MacDonald would share Benjamin's diagnosis that the result of massive reproduction is "the contemporary decay of the aura." According to Benjamin, this is a product of two circumstances, both of which are related to the increasing significance of the masses in contemporary life. Namely, the desire of contemporary masses to bring things "closer" spatially and humanly, which is just as ardent as their bent toward overcoming the uniqueness of every reality by accepting its reproduction.

Inseparable from the abandonment of aura is the "sense of the universal equality of things." Here, Benjamin is anticipating postmodernism and its undermining of the notion of the real, as in the French social critic Jean Baudrillard's theory of simulacrum, in which there is no longer any distinction between reality and its representation. Baudrillard, however, would consider Benjamin's analysis obsolete because it relies on what he calls the second order of simulacra, which took place with the industrial revolution of the nineteenth century, when mass production and the ability to create copies broke down the distinctions between the image and the representation. We now, Baudrillard claims, live in the third order of simulacra, where the representation precedes and determines the real; it becomes a substitute rather than a copy.

In Baudrillard's theory of simulacrum there is no longer any distinction between reality and its representation.

When I was a boy going to Saturday matinee Westerns, my cartoon watching was limited to one a week—Bugs or Porky or Donald. It was a special treat for my prepubescent self. Now, if I chose (and I don't), I could turn on the Cartoon Network and find myself glutted with animation 24/7.

And in 1960, when, instead of talking to Alexa, I was sitting at a table in the smoke-filled Five Spot as John Coltrane performed "Wise One" live, I was enveloped by a unique event—seeing the tensions in Coltrane's face, the angle of his horn, the movements of his fingers. Not just being in the Five Spot; experiencing a version of "Wise One" unlike any performance before and after. Alexa brings up just one performance of many and locks it in an unchanging digital code. Yet, all I have to do is ask, any time, day or night. Convenience at the price of aura? Beyond that, does the relentless availability invite distraction?

Ultimately, I find myself less convinced by Benjamin's—and MacDonald's—arguments that reproductions undermine and ultimately debase the integrity of art than I am by the political aspects of Benjamin's analysis.

MacDonald today comes across as a snob, the firm distinctions he makes are obsolete in an age in which the best products of so-called popular culture are considered works of art; where jazz is played at New York's home for classical music, Lincoln Center; where artists themselves have taken over the technology of mechanical reproduction for their own creative purposes. And, while I can hear a contemporary performance of Beethoven's Eroica symphony in a concert hall, my only access to the music of the late John Coltrane is through a recording.

At stake for Benjamin is the role of reproduced art in the social and political destruction of his time.

What I consider more political than artistic is the blurring of entertainment, news, and politics that is exacerbated by the plethora of digital reproduction techniques. The sad epitome of this trend in 2018 may be found in the U.S. President, a one-time TV personality who is obsessed with the simulacra of "Fox and Friends," who confuses governing with contesting in a game show, who measures success by audience size, and who appears to value applause over substance. Rather than a unique phenomenon, Trump may be considered the epitome of a society that values celebrity and entertainment, i.e., distraction, over substance.

Benjamin's analysis does explain how Trump is abetted by our immersion in a realm of reproduction. For Benjamin, those representations are apprehended according to current ideology rather than an independent aesthetic or intellectual standard.

He considers politics the source of such ideology: As a result, the relationship to a work of art for those he calls "the masses"—you and me—is transformed from one of concentration to distraction. Such distraction is a form of "covert control." When the masses face a "task" they would rather avoid, reproduced art will provide an escape. Writing in 1935, Benjamin put his emphasis on movies as the art form that caters to our need for distraction. Today he might accuse the panoply of digital outlets in front of our eyes or plugged into our ears.

For those today who have not fallen prey to political propaganda, the ease of indulging in such distractions may make them accomplices in the undermining of liberal democracy, humanism, and evidence-based decision-making. The ubiquitous replications of video, music, and the visual provide seductive distractions. Some ignore all but the most blatant headlines. Others lose themselves consuming media that parrots what they already believe.

Our mechanical-digital technology makes it easier than ever for wealthy governments, corporations, and individuals to control masses of people. News of Russian hacking and of Cambridge Analytica's manipulations have made many want to fight back. But are we indeed able to resist the power of methods and forces we may not even know exist and that seek to distract us into obliviousness?

John Coltrane's "Wise One" is a work of beauty. Would that a simple request would produce wise ones to save us from the manipulating despots and would-be despots.

Endnotes

[1] That is, the devaluing of tradition bodes cultural and political ruin.
[2] Elsewhere he writes: "During long periods of history, the mode of human sense perception changes with humanity's entire mode of existence. The manner in which human sense perception is organized, the medium in which it is accomplished, is determined not only by nature but by historical circumstances as well."

Sources

Walter Benjamin. *The Work of Art in the Age of Mechanical Reproduction.* Translated by Harry Zohn.
Dino Felluga. *Modules on Baudrillard.*

Dwight MacDonald. Excerpts from "A Theory of Mass Culture" by Dwight MacDonald, in *Diogenes*, No. 3, Summer 1953, pp. 1-17.

YouTube. *Quest—Every Movie.*

Bird in Words

MUSIC IS A SELF-CONTAINED LANGUAGE, often powerful
and moving, but perhaps beyond translation. Saxophon-
ist Joshua Redman emphasizes this point when com-
menting on Ken Burn 's TV documentary *Jazz*, quoting
Matt Glaser: "Music expresses things that cannot be
expressed any other way. Then you attempt to find language to describe that, the words fall short."

Martin Gray has taken the challenge of that attempt
in *Blues for Bird*, a twelve-book epic on the life and art
of Charlie Parker, the horn player who transformed jazz
in the middle of the twentieth century and at the same
time destroyed himself with heroin and alcohol, both
musical genius and strung-out addict through a life of
thirty-four frenetic years. And he took a number of
other players with him by his example, the illusion that
drugs and brilliant solos were inseparable. Certainly, the
life of such a shattered giant compels literary expression,
words that capture what Clint Eastwood sought on film
with his movie *Bird*. But Eastwood had the advantage of
a soundtrack.

Gray complicates his task by using poetry rather
than fiction or biographical narrative. In fact, the biog-
raphies and musical histories of other writers are his
sources, and he has dug deeply in the facts and lore of
Parker's life, as well as the commentaries of musicians
and musicologists. *Blues for Bird* shows the results of

thorough research in its richness of information about Parker's life and his impact on jazz. By referring to this material so frequently and directly, Gray set himself a dual task of translation—finding words for music and turning prose statements into poetic form.

For example, as an appendix to Book IV, "Bird Discovers Bop," he provides the full text of the source he used for poems XXIX and XXX, page 112 of Ross Russell's *Bird Lives*. Russell's sentences, "Charlie's entrance, after Minor's erratic trumpet solo, is dashing and self-assured. Playing in perfect time, he constructs a line from a series of meticulously dotted eighth and sixteenth notes, throwing in an occasional gruppetto, a la Lester Young" to become:

> On Minor's errant horn
> Charlie's entry is dashing, self-assured.
> Played in perfect time
> he constructs a line
> from dotted eighths, sixteenths
> which is meticulous
> and throws *gruppettos* in
> a la Lester Young.

As in this poem, each of *Blues for Bird*'s 5,665 lines is cast in iambic trimeter, a meter that Gray explained in an article about the poem as his "attempt to reflect jazz rhythms, especially the beat and offbeat movement within bop."

Clearly a knowledgeable and passionate jazz fan, Gray also brought to his effort an extensive record as a scholar, with four books about Tennyson, and a poet, with a 120-page work on Jackson Pollock, *Memories Arrested in Space*. Not only did Pollock cause a revolution in painting during the same years Parker remade music, they died a year apart, Parker in 1955, Pollock in 1956, and both were extraordinary personalities—larger than life in their creativity and self-destructiveness. But painting itself is a much more hospitable subject for poetry than music, with words to express the shapes, forms, and subjects visible to the eye, a slash of red, a bowl of oranges. A writer can make us see Pollock. Can Gray make us hear Parker?

Book I of *Blues for Bird*, "Parker at His Peak," reveals Gray's epic goal with *Aeneid*-like opening lines that echo "Arms, and the man I sing" from John Dryden's seventeenth-century translation of Virgil's original Latin "Arma virumque cano":

> Sax and the man I sing
> Yes, man and saxophone—
> how Charlie Parker rose
> from Kansas City ground
> to learn to play his horn
> till he was better than
> the best man who could play
> the alto saxophone.

Parker's armory was his instrument, not Aeneas's sword, and rather than building "majestic Rome," he created a majestic music. To pursue the analogy, one might consider heroin his Dido, his seductive temptation, one that he—unlike Aeneas—could not forsake. Some—especially considering the musicians who followed Parker into addiction—might consider his slavery to heroin the equivalent to the pact with the devil made by Thomas Mann's Adrian Leverkühn in *Doctor Faustus*, the sacrifice for creative powers. Mann's novel, published in 1947 at the peak of Parker's career, is another literary work rooted in music, the life story of a fictitious German composer whose twelve-tone musical theories Mann borrowed from Arnold Schoenberg.

Evocation of music is essential to Mann's goals for his novel; the reader must have a vivid sense of his hero's creations. One example of the manner used by Mann to describe Leverkühn's music is this passage by the story's narrator, Serenus Zeitblom, about a piece called "Apocalypse": ". . . The theme represented by howling— what horror! And what acoustic panic results from the repeated drum-glissandos, an effect made possible on the chromatic or machine drum by changing the tuning to various pitches during the drum-roll. The effect is extremely uncanny. But most shattering of all is the application of the glissando to the human voice, which after all was the first target in organizing the tonic material and ridding song of its primitive howling over several notes: the return, in short, to this primitive stage . . ."

Mann succeeds by merging the technical details of musicology with several emotionally charged interpretive details through words like "howling," "horror," "shattering," and "primitive."

Mann's evocations are made in the rhythms of prose, as translated by H.T. Lowe-Porter. Gray's poetry uses a similar strategy of mixing terms of performance with an unsettling vocabulary to describe the classic "Parker's Mood" in poem XXVIII of Book I, "Parker at His Peak":

In Parker's Mood you hear
the saxophone alone
backed by the rhythm group.
It is a classic blues
just like *The Hootie Blues*
Slam Slam Blues, Cool Blues
and also *Now's The Time*.
Plunges are headlong and
descents prodigious
full of slides and slurs
with notes intensified
by deft false fingerings.
Its panoramic sound
suggest an empire's reign
before its long decline.

The litany of titles leads into an emotionally charged vocabulary: "plunges," "descents prodigious," "slide and slurs," "deft false fingerings," and "decline." While Mann's thematic concern is a darker vision of the world, a cataclysm, Gray uses his charged words to illuminate the music, merging the terms of descent with a metaphoric allusion to Parker's personal fate.

In jazz, a more familiar attempt to put music into words is called *vocalese*, the lyrics given to classic jazz solos by singers like Eddie Jefferson and King Pleasure. In this case, the voice serves as an instrument that duplicates the solo's notes using words that seek to interpret its mood. King Pleasure gave these to the beginning of "Parker's Mood":

Come with me if you wanna go to Kansas City
I'm feelin' low-down and blue
My heart's full of sorrow
Don't hardly know what to do
Where will I be tomorrow?

At the time this record was released, Parker was in serious mental and physical decline. Not only was the tune pirated with no reward to Parker from its large sales, as Gray puts it:

The lyric prophesied
Bird's death was imminent . . .
The obscene lyric of
Bird's tune King Pleasure
occurring like a curse
to blight Bird's final year
and taint his latter days.

Mann's Leverkühn died seated at his piano, surrounded by the women in his life and Zeitblom, his hands falling on the keys "in a strangely dissonant chord." Then, "At the same time he opened his mouth as though to sing, but only a wail which will ring for ever in my ears broke from his lips. He spread out his arms, bending over the instrument and seeming about to embrace it, when suddenly, as though smitten by a blow, he fell sidewise from his seat and to the floor."

Parker died in the Park Lane suite of Baroness Pannonica "Nica" de Koenigswarter, a European-born patron of jazz musicians, who later tended to Thelonious Monk in his decline. Parker had been drinking, in his words, "about a quart a day" and in his last moments sat in front of the television set. This is how Gray describes his death in poem XXI of Book XII "Bird's Memorial":

Bird uttered his last words
as he watched a music show:
'what a wonderful trombone!'
Praise was on his lips
praise that was musical
when drawing his last breath.
He then began to choke
while laughing at an act
and fell back in his chair.

Gray's basic method is understatement, almost straight reporting. No ever-ringing wail breaking from Charlie Parker's lips. But Gray does report that the baroness heard a thunderclap as the moment of death passed, and she asks, 'Was God receiving Bird / or Bird knocking at the Gate?'

Parker is just one of the jazz musicians, artists, and forms that comprise the subjects of Dan Jaffe's *Playing the Word: Jazz Poems*. Like Gray, Jaffe seeks a language that embodies the feel of the music and the life of those who make the music. Jaffe makes it his goal to merge poetry and jazz. Each poem must be "true to the jazz experience . . . It's not enough that it be about jazz. It must be jazz." He speaks of stops and starts, the click of fricatives, the lushness of vowels, all working to capture the feel and sound of the music.

This collection appears in five parts, dedications to and evocations of many musicians, particularly those from Kansas City, where Jaffe spent many years—some well-known figures like Sonny Rollins and Mingus and Monk, others local celebrities. One section—"them blues"—is dedicated to that form, a series that emulates the lyrics and moods of painful loss expressed in the hurt of old-time blues. Parker, alone of jazz players, has a section—"bopping with Bird"—devoted to him.

While Gray adheres to a single poetic form for his epic, Jaffe chooses a range of rhythms and forms for the speakers of his words—Parker's mother, his wife, Bird himself, Jaffe as poet. This flexibility allows him to seek sounds that capture the variety of Parker's improvisations. Gray tends to be more factually narrative in his descriptions, Jaffe more allusive, more playful in his language, as in "Yardbird": "In the alley / alongside / or out back / behind the dumpster / or in the gravel pit / next to the window well / he keeps peckin' / driving his beak/ at the hard stuff / of the world. When you can't hear / he's behind the shed / out of range / or teaching worms / how to crawl / practicing / some low tune / later you'll hear / what you can't / even then you / won't know quite / what Yardbird's done."

Jaffe gives us Parker's wit in words put into Bird's mouth in "Bird Talks After Bellevue":

> Sometime I get an idea
> and try it. When I look at my fingers
> I'm surprised it's me.

Or his own words in a report of Parker's funeral in "Unveiling the Bird":

His notes spin off through the air
Like late November leaves.

Ultimately Gray and Jaffe take different approaches to the life and music of Charlie Parker, Jaffe offering eleven short poems like a session of brief improvisations, rich and rhythmic, that touch the core of the man and his playing. Gray's epic gives us the life in full, the arc of Parker's creation and his destruction.

As much as he succeeds in portraying Parker's tormented life and the wonder of his art, ultimately, Gray cannot make us hear Parker. No words can translate into sound beyond their own inherent music. But *Blues for Bird* certainly can lead us to the music it celebrates. Most of the poem's readers will probably already know the music, the words evoking it from their memories—"Koko," "Ornithology," "Scrapple from the Apple," "Cool Blues." For such readers the experience will be enriched, deepened by testimonies to its greatness and by the sufferings of the man who made it.

Sources

Martin Gray, *Blues for Bird*. Santa Monica, CA: Santa Monica Press, 2001.

Dan Jaffe, *Playing the Word: Jazz Poems*. Kansas City: BkMk Press, 2001.

Seeing and Believing

"Seeing is believing" according to the familiar adage. More accurately, "Seeing is believing what we think we see."

At a recent writing workshop I joined an exercise to write about a painting, choosing Rembrandt's "Old Man with a Gold Chain." I put my "reading" into words: "Half a face, just one eye gazing out, the other lost in a dark shadow. Black dominates. Even the gold chain is barely visible. Is the insignificance of the chain a commentary on the insignificance of material wealth?"

Now, I knew the Dutch had enjoyed a bonanza of wealth during Rembrandt's lifetime. That was the Dutch Golden Age, a period flush with the profits of trade and indulgence in conspicuous consumption. Thus, I found myself puzzled why he could have been so blatant in his dismissal of riches. But the painting's reproduction lay right in front of me, the title chain barely visible against the black of the old man's garment.

After jotting our comments, we were instructed to use our wi-fi devices to find online information about the painting we had chosen. The reproduction that appeared on my screen startled me. It was so very different from the print I had been interpreting. Not only was the man's face fully illuminated, the chain dominated the center of the work, the gold heavy and opulent.

Even though this version was yet another reproduction, I had to assume it was much closer to the original work, because it was clearer and because it fulfilled my assumptions about the Dutch Golden Age. The print that had misled me so drastically was obviously the product of faulty printing. Yet it was a widely sold reproduction, and I must have been one of thousands who failed to experience the "real" Rembrandt. And, in my case, come to a wildly wrong interpretation.

Then it stuck me that I hadn't been subjected to a one-off. There must be thousands of poorly printed art reproductions and even shades of difference in those of high quality. We look at such prints many times more than we view originals.

How many of our artistic perceptions are inaccurate? And how do we define an accurate perception? Is my "accurate" perception, your "accurate" perception? What does it mean to really see a painting?

The art critic John Berger takes on this question in his 1992 work, *Ways of Seeing*, opening the book with a section that he acknowledges borrows heavily on Walter Benjamin's "The Work of Art in an Age of Mechanical Reproduction."

One matter Berger considers by implication is whether I can ever—if I traveled to the Chicago Art Institute—see the Rembrandt original without the context of my blunder. Writing of another reproduction, he says, ". . . the uniqueness of the original now lies in it being the original of a reproduction. It is no longer what its image shows that strikes one as unique; its first meaning is no longer to be found in what it says, but in what it is."

Berger also believes the context and placement of a reproduction—along with our background of viewing works of art—determines the way we regard the work:

"What we make of that painted moment when it is before our eyes depends upon what we expect of art, and that in turn depends today upon how we have already experienced the meaning of painting through reproductions."

I suppose in my case, beyond my initial distortion of the Dutch past, my focus has been on the inadequate reproduction, with the Rembrandt painting itself just a pawn for my assignment. But even if in the future I stood before the original, I wouldn't really be seeing it, my perception skewed by my memory of the bad reproduction as well as by the reverent artificiality of the museum setting.

This artificiality, according to Berger, shouldn't be considered a phenomenon of public collections in monumental settings. He finds a version of such an attitude in the origin of oil painting, where the possession of such a painting in a private home was itself a status symbol more than it was a tribute to artistic excellence.

Even though oil pigments had existed for centuries, Berger dates the dominance of oil painting to the sixteenth century and finds that the medium still informs our cultural assumptions about viewing works of art and defining "artistic genius." At the same time, its value is inseparable from possession of the work itself.

Berger argues that the "art of any period tends to serve the ideological interests of the ruling class." Between 1500 and 1900, oil painting provided the ideal visual medium to depict a new way of seeing the world though its attitudes to property and exchange. The unique ability of oil painting to render the solidity of its subjects offers the illusion of objects filling a space, "filling a world." The owners of such paintings were really displaying their power over the objects of the world around them by bringing them inside to hang on their walls.

While rarely using the gold leaf common in medieval art, "many oil paintings were themselves simple demonstrations of what gold or money could buy. Merchandise became the actual subject-matter of works of art."

Thus, the gold chain I failed to see clearly in the poor reproduction of the Rembrandt painting. Yet, if Berger is right, I may have blundered onto an insight despite my misinterpretation. Rather than the belt, the painting itself has become the real object of conspicuous consumption. I couldn't Google the value of "Old Man with a Gold Chain," but in 2009 another Rembrandt oil sold for more than $33 million at a London auction. Despite the barely seen gold chain, I was looking at the copy of an object of immense worth.

Sources

John Berger. *Ways of Seeing.* Penguin, 1992.

Photographing the Soul

A review of *The Iconic Photographs* by Steve McCurry
(Phaidon reprint edition, 2012; first published by Art
and Architecture, 2011)

TWO-THIRDS INTO STEVE McCURRY's *Iconic Photo-graphs* collection I thought I was encountering a group
of happy men, their smiling faces lined in a row. Then
I realized those smiles were painted-on masks, not real
expressions. The photo's title is "Young Wadair Men,
Niger 1986," and the explanatory note at the end of the
book reveals that these young men were participating
in an annual tribal ritual of dancing for hours to attract
brides with exaggerated made-up looks that revealed
nothing of person beneath them, only guises of artificial
joy.

What made me especially alert to these seeming
smiles was a photograph several pages before the Wadair
men in which one brightly costumed girl, a Cambodi-
an dancer, tilts her head and displays what I took to be
youthful happiness. It hadn't occurred to me till then that
in the dozens of photographs up to that point solemnity
dominated. The faces, young and old, stare directly at
the camera, the young often seemingly startled or fearful, their elders weathered and almost defiant, inured
to hardship. The dancer's smile stood out, and I began
looking for more.

Of course, I'm reading the photographs, possibly imposing meanings preconditioned by my assumptions about the areas where McCurry found his subjects. *Iconic Photographs* contains 244 pictures, the great majority taken in Asia and some in Africa. His picture-taking travels included Nepal, Afghanistan, India, Bangladesh, Tibet, Burma, Pakistan, Cambodia, Mali, and Yemen, countries in which many people live in extreme poverty, some of the countries long locked in civil war. In addition to close-ups of individual faces, the collection includes people in the midst of landscapes, many of these people shown doing arduous work or surrounded by scenes of destitution.

Was I seeing what I expected to see? Did McCurry select people and scenes that reinforced such preconditioning? How much are the looks on people's faces reactions to being photographed, and by an outsider? Do these expressions tell us much more about the photographic process than about the people?

Certainly, in some of the group scenes and those with humans in the midst of urban and natural environments, it's likely that people didn't know they were being photographed. But I wonder about the many close-ups of faces, where the camera must have been so close that the subjects couldn't have been unaware. How camera-conscious were they?

In many ways the photograph of the young Wadair men is emblematic of the whole of McCurry's book—artistic design applied to ambiguous realities. A question arises. Is McCurry with his excellent photographer's eye "falsifying" these people and the settings in which they must live, perhaps even to the degree of unconscious exploitation for the sake of a picture? Or is he revealing an essential dignity in their existences and in their manner of living, a triumph of endurance?

Many awards, including Magazine Photographer of the Year, attest to McCurry's status as a significant photographer. A round sticker on the dust jacket of *Iconic Images* announces that McCurry's collection was "Awarded Judges Special Recognition Pictures of the Year International Best Photography Book Award." Just opening the cover and viewing a few examples led me to validate the judges. These are remarkable photographs, with great aesthetic beauty in their design and use of brilliant colors. But what does such design have to do with the actual subjects being designed? Has McCurry produced works of art rather than works of social-economic verisimilitude?

Although he has published photographs in many magazines, McCurry is most associated with *The National Geographic*, perhaps the result of a single cover photo of an Afghan refugee girl the magazine's website calls "a high point in McCurry's career . . . that many have described as the most recognizable photograph in the world today." Some believe *National Geographic* imposes its editorial perspective of imposing a comfortable view of life on the entire world. Its web page on McCurry credits him for capturing "the essence of human struggle and joy" and notes that he realized, "If you wait, people will forget your camera and the soul will drift up into view."

While many may still consider photography to be an "innocent" art, an objective depiction of what's out there, whether it be people or place, many analyses have deconstructed that notion. Photography, like painting and literature, is a selective art, the result of many choices—camera angle, boundaries, lighting, exposure, what's included and what's excluded, the number of shots discarded before one is chosen. I don't know about McCurry's processes—how he frames, how he chooses, how he selects, how he edits, how he decides he has captured the "soul." Even with the unlikely possibility that he just points and shoots, the results would be just momentary glimpses.

We appreciate a good photograph as we do a good painting, poem, story, or novel. These arts provide a fulfilling aesthetic vision of life that is ultimately self-contained, shaping the inchoate world outside the work. Through selection artists produce artifacts rather than reports. Of course, a photograph also conveys a sense, right or wrong, that it is closer to reality than configurations of painted colors or of words. The phenomenon of news photography reinforces this assumption. We'd like to believe we can know what is truly happening.

McCurry's art is especially convincing, particularly when it fulfills expectations, at least of someone like me who knows about the worlds of his subjects only through what he has heard, read, or seen before in print and on TV. McCurry's dominant treatment of people and places depicts things as I thought they would be in regions of poverty. Walls are cracked and crumbling, pillars chipped, layers missing. Streets are surrounded by heaps of rubble, in some cases the result of bombing, in most others just decay. Old cars are battered shells, landscapes often dark, obscured by smoke and steam. Street scenes reveal a jumble of signs, carts, food stands, battered buildings, and shabby people. Beggars sleep in streets. Workers stagger under burdens.

In those few photographs that include examples of middle-class life or Western brands, the results are ironic. A young monk in a teashop in Bodh Gaya, India, sits under a huge Coca-Cola sign that dominates the top half of the picture. A young businessman in Mumbai sits for shoe repair among the ragged cobblers in an open-air shop by the railroad station, his white shirt and tie placed in the exact center of the photograph. Shirtless men paint publicity signs for Bollywood films, the faces of the stars much larger than those of the living painters.

Occasional pictures of tranquility relieve these views of deterioration and adversity. People pray. A white-bearded man in white robes sits while a boy, perhaps a grandson, also in white, sleeps against him. While a standing woman prays, seated male monks in Tibet smile (another rare example of smiling), the monks and the woman seemingly oblivious of each other. At the Holi festival in Rajasthan, India, a man in a state of reverie is carried aloft through the crowd on a sea of turbans. The colors of these turbans, like those of the monks' robes and so much of the clothing and objects throughout the book, are bright and vibrant.

Ultimately what McCurry offers in these "iconic" photographs are images that suggest that human existence is richly complex. Have he and his camera revealed in the midst of the seemingly severe lives "the essence of human struggle and joy"? Would another photographer in the same places and seeing the same people have produced photographs of defeat and misery? At the least, McCurry's talent results in aesthetic satisfactions.

A Bendel Bonnet,
A Shakespeare Sonnet

WHAT DO A BENDEL BONNET and a Shakespeare son-net have in common besides rhyme? Throw in Mickey Mouse. No, it's not a riddle manqué or a question reject-ed by the Miller Analogies test. As many probably know already, these are just a few of the superlative attributes applied to the person who is nonpareil in Cole Porter's 1934 song "You're the Top." In fact, the list of best-in-kind comparisons goes on for verse after verse, including the Mona Lisa, the Tower of Pisa, Mahatma Gandhi, Napoleon brandy, cellophane, an O'Neill drama, a Wal-dorf salad, Whistler's mama, and camembert. While the wit of this compilation is yet another example of Porter's lyrical brilliance, it may also be considered symptomatic of a tectonic shift in the hierarchy of cultural values that took place in the early twentieth century.

The song was written for the musical *Anything Goes*, with a Porter title song that's yet another indication of an upheaval:

> The world's gone mad today
> And good's bad today
> And black's white today
> And day's night today

Porter uses the word "shocking" in the song, and

many people were shocked by jazz, art deco, dada, and surrealism, not just by "a glimpse of stocking."

"You're the Top" contains, in effect, a cultural blurring, a fashionable hat given equal value to the poetry of Shakespeare. What would Matthew Arnold have said? Would he have rolled over in his 1888 grave? Arnold introduced the term "high culture" in his 1869 book *Culture and Anarchy*, defining it as "the disinterested endeavour after man's perfection" pursued, obtained, and achieved by an effort to "know the best that has been said and thought in the world."

For Arnold, if he had written a version of "You're the Top," all of the comparatives would have been examples such as Goethe's *Faust*, Plato's *Phaedo*, *Oedipus Rex*, and, of course—like Porter, Shakespeare's sonnets. As his book's title indicates, the opposite and enemy of culture is anarchy, which he considers lacks standards and a sense of direction. He associates anarchy with England's growing moves toward democracy in the second half of the nineteenth century. No doubt, he would have considered Porter's lyrics an example of such anarchy—"the world's gone mad today." Or to use lines from Arnold's own poem "Dover Beach":

> And we are here as on a darkling plain
> Swept with confused alarms of struggle and flight,
> Where ignorant armies clash by night.

The late twentieth century attacks on the literary canon—an exalted list of works almost all by dead white males—can be considered an anti-Arnold movement, Arnold himself being one of the dead white males.

Beyond ignoring works by women and people from minority groups, the canon was based on the assumption that some experts had the authority to determine the best that had been said and thought and objective standards existed for making such judgments.

Might "You're the Top" be a whimsical version of a new canon? If not, the specific choices in the list might serve as a strategy way to deconstruct the old canon?

Yet, even thirty years after Porter, a defender of Arnoldian standards can be found in Dwight Mac-Donald, a journalist and cultural critic who mixed a patrician background—Phillips Exeter and Yale—with radical politics as a writer for *The New Yorker*. He probably is best known for his delineation of culture that compares high culture to the lesser qualities of what he called Masscult and Midcult in the title of a 1960 *Partisan Review* essay.

For him, works of high cultural value called for an active engagement of the reader or observer and produced sophisticated emotional and intellectual reactions. Masscult works are essentially prepackaged and easy to access, emotionally lazy. Midcult he found more dangerous in its pretentious mixture of high and mass culture, seemingly sophisticated but still accessible with minimal thinking. In that category, he placed works like Hemingway's *The Old Man and the Sea* and the writing of John Steinbeck. Would MacDonald have categorized Porter Mid- or Mass-?

Ironically, a magazine he wrote for, *The New Yorker*, has been put down as Midcult in distinction to, say, *The New York Review of Books*, clearly high culture. The circulation of the former is roughly a million and a quarter, that of the latter 135,000, about one-tenth as large. *The New Yorker* launched in 1925, five years before *Anything Goes*, and might be considered an example of a cultural potpourri mixed in the pages of a publication—cartoons, humor writing, fiction by excellent writers, profiles of a variety of people and subjects, and advertisements for expensive products.

In a representative issue, the one of November 24, 1934, three days after *Anything Goes* opened on Broadway, a reader could find—amid many cartoons and pages of ads for products ranging from Dewar's Scotch, the new Hupmobile, Beech-Nut chewing gum, to Lucky Strikes—a short story by Norman Matson, humor by Robert Benchley, a poem by Ogden Nash, a profile of the Kewpie doll, a book review by Clifton Fadiman, a movie review of the Astaire-Rogers *The Gay Divorcee*, reviews of music and art galleries, and articles on sports and fashions.

A magazine with a similar cultural mix that thrived from the teens through the 1930s was the original *Vanity Fair*. Its issue of the *Anything Goes* month of November 1934 featured a caricature of Franklin Delano Roosevelt on the cover, with an internal conglomeration including a short story by Alan Seager, H.L. Mencken's "Why Not an American Monarchy?," John Gunther writing about the exiled Archduke Otto, Marquis W. Childs on the wicked city of New Orleans, and an article on the shopping bazaars of Manhattan, Bendel's counterparts.

If there were a competition between Porter and MacDonald, Porter is the clear winner, the ranking of cultural values no longer pertinent. In fact, in many ways, Masscult has become the source of new form of mythological references. Consider Mickey Mouse, one of the superlatives defining the person who is the Top, and the cute rodent's recognition throughout the world. In fact, the cartoon character was once rated the most famous symbol of America.

Yet many references of the literary works in the canon require detailed footnoting to explain names and terms contemporary readers would have understood immediately. The Porter song, too, close to ninety years old now, contains names and objects that would escape many younger listeners today—the nose of the great Durante, Garbo's salary, and no doubt a Bendel bonnet. A Henri Bendel hat was considered the height of fashion in the 1930s, examples displayed in the high culture Metropolitan Museum of Art. But the store he founded in 1895 on the New York Fifth Avenue site of a Vanderbilt mansion closed forever in 2019.

Still, such ephemera plays a greater cultural role in recent writing than, say, Phoebus Apollo. Brand names—the products characters own or covet—serve as shorthands to define their personal tastes and economic, educational, and social status. An author can avoid paragraphs of exposition just by writing whether a character drives a Tesla or a sputtering Toyota Corolla, drinks Bud Light or Châteauneuf-du-Pape, reads *The New Yorker* or *The New York Review*, or eats flown-in Omaha Steaks or SPAM.

SPAM became the one-word lyric of a Monty Python song and the term to designate the junk that arrives on a computer because of the hash of unlikely ingredients blended into that canned meat product.

Another canned-meat product may mark a cultural turning point in the literary merger of high culture and Masscult references. That's James Joyce's 1922 novel, *Ulysses*, based on Homer's *Odyssey* transplanted to twentieth-century Dublin. Plumtree's Potted Meat and its advertising jingle runs through the mind of the novel's protagonist, Leopold Bloom, a seller of commercial advertising space, who associates the product with the newly buried body of Paddy Dignam, the haunting memory of his dead son, Rudy, and the adulterous relationship of Bloom's wife, Molly, with Blazes Boylan. The term "to pot one's meat" is Irish slang for copulation.

Ironically, the singer of accolades to the person who rates as the Top has an almost masochist self-evaluation: "Baby, I'm the bottom, you're the top." If Bloom had been singing the song, he might tell Molly she was a Homeric heroine and himself mere potential potted meat.

If such a Bloom had been thinking of a Shakespeare sonnet, it would, unfortunately, be the line, "An expense of spirit in a waste of shame" rather than, "Let me not to the marriage of true minds / Admit impediments."

Cole Porter may have been having a sport when he wrote "You're the Top," but, as Adam Gopnik writes about him in *The New Yorker*, "He takes pleasure in rhyme for rhyme's sake, in the play of language, and does so in a way that is, oddly, far more in tune with the main lines of the American avant-garde of his time than operetta style could ever be."

Matthew Arnold and high culture have followed the fate of Paddy Dignam. The world's gone mad today.

Bongo, Bongo, Bongo: The Other as Cartoon and Caricature

NOW THAT WE LIVE IN A TIME OF 24/7 NEWS and video from every nook and cranny of the planet, we're constantly exposed to the sinister side of human civilization, the hearts of darkness in cities, villages, and countrysides—beheadings, bodies in mass graves, suicide bombings, conflagrations of all sorts. But I recall the seeming innocence of a much less informed time, when international news reports were scarce and the world out there could be regarded as an amusing phenomenon.

Take the Democratic Republic of Congo, most recently in the news because of a disputed presidential election, those in power apparently awarding victory to a man who may have received fewer votes. In a larger context, that's a mild disagreement for a land where six million people have died from the ravages of civil wars and diseases like Ebola, where the potential of rich mineral wealth makes internal corruption rampant and a lure for the manipulations of multinational corporations seeking riches like rare earths for digital devices. A form of neo-colonialism has replaced the original colonial occupation, including gleaning profits from selling the munitions that caused the deaths of many of those millions. This Congo is the setting for Nobel laureate V.S. Naipaul's grim 1979 novel, *A Bend in the River*, and decades before that, in 1899, Joseph Conrad's *Heart of Darkness*.

I first read Conrad's haunting novella in the 1950s with no real knowledge of the country nor of the brutal history of Belgian occupation. For me, the story took place in an African somewhere amid an impenetrable tangle of jungle, where a brilliant white European went mad and put severed heads on poles. The horror. My reading took place during the time of duck-and-cover in America, kids crouched under desks as feeble protection from a nuclear explosion. The atom bomb was the terror of the time, not machetes.

It was also the period of the song "Civilization (Bongo, Bongo, Bongo)" written in 1947, two years after Hiroshima and Nagasaki:

> So bongo, bongo, bongo, I don't wanna leave the Congo, oh
> no no no no no
> Bingo, bangle, bungle, I'm so happy in the jungle, I refuse
> to go
> Don't want no bright lights, false teeth, doorbells, land
> lords, I make it clear
> That no matter how they coax me, I'll stay right here

And concluding:

> They have things like the atom bomb, so I think I'll stay
> where I ahm
> Civilization, I'll stay right here!

The song's Congo was, of course, a comic book escape from the civilization in which our most brilliant scientific minds had produced a heart of darkness potentially looming over our heads. And so popular songs gave us the fantasy of an unthreatening innocence out there.

For another happy escape, consider "Managua, Nicaragua," from the year before "Civilization," 1946, containing the lyrical couplet:

> Managua, Nicaragua, what a wonderful spot
> There's coffee and bananas and a temperature hot

Of course, today Managua is a city to avoid, where the country's violent unrest leads citizens to rush to the passport office in hope of fleeing.

And back in 1945, the calypso song "Rum and Coca-Cola" promised that if, instead, you ever went down to Trinidad:

> They make you feel so very glad
> Calypso sing and make up rhyme
> Guarantee you one real good fine time

Back then, when the little-known world—other countries—wasn't being portrayed as ripe for naïve escape, it embodied comic foolishness, as in 1946's "The Coffee Song," which gave us the line "They grow an awful lot of coffee in Brazil." In one stanza:

> The politician's daughter
> Was accused of drinking water
> And was fined a great big fifty dollar bill

In another song of the period, "The Maharajah of

Madagor," from 1948, the maharajah is willing to give up his rubies and pearls and loveliest girls for dance lessons because, although he was exceedingly rich, "But he didn't know how to do the rumba."

Not only were Americans in the years of these songs fearful of the atom bomb, they were still recovering from World War II, overwhelmed by news of devastated Europe, suffering deprivations at home, and seeing reminders of American war deaths in gold star windows. The framing of the world beyond our borders as exotic playgrounds or lands of folly was a new way of minimizing the significance of others, especially non-Europeans.

This dismissal of others grows from the belief in American exceptionalism and its roots in the assumption of Anglo-Saxon superiority. Of course, even though nations and cultures share a long history of belittling outsiders—and this has included making those in neighboring countries the targets of ethnic jokes—that's a step away from denying their humanity.

Colonialism—and now neo-colonialism—has assumed the inferiority of the native population, people of different skin tones, clothing, diets, customs, and belief systems. If they were too ignorant to live according to right and proper standards, they must be inadequate, existing only to serve the more advanced civilization as workers and sources of wealth. In fact, accepting their worth would undermine the essential premises of colonialism and the right to exploit those who were not like "us."

While usually unstated, that assumption may be seen in Victorian novels, where characters like Jos Sedley in Thackeray's *Vanity Fair* return from colonial service with a financial hoard but little acknowledgment of the foreign places in which they had lived. That's especially evident in Dickens' *Great Expectations*, when Pip, shattered by disappointment in love and self-regard, and deep in debt, spends eleven years in Egypt employed as a clerk and then partner in a mercantile firm. Those years don't matter. The two paragraphs Dickens gives them summarize an absent blank, life outside of England being meaningless.

At the same time, readers were curious about what lay out there in the midst of remoteness. Thus, the many works that described travel to foreign lands where the climate, customs, and people were bizarre and strange, oddities worth knowing about but certainly not as destinations for living, unless one was a transported convict or a penniless son far down in the family line.

That curiosity led to the fabrications of the exotic, which particularly involved a fascination with "Arabia," after the great popularity of the tales in *One Thousand and One Nights*. Genies, magic carpets, and talking serpents, along with fantasies of Tahitian lushness and the like, offered an antidote to the mundane.

Yet while reading about the antics of these distant characters might have been amusing, you certainly didn't want to bring such people home. One disturbing example found in a novel by a Dickens contemporary is the mixed European and Caribbean heritage of Bertha Mason, whom Mr. Rochester in Charlotte Brontë's *Jane Eyre* married in Jamaica. Bertha turns out to be "gross, impure, depraved" and a lunatic to be locked away on Rochester's Thornfield estate, the archetypal madwoman in the attic. As if contact with the Caribbean isn't bad enough, at the end of the novel, Jane's hyper-religious cousin, St. John Rivers, is dying in India, marked by his failure to convert and civilize the natives.

Charlotte Brontë's sister Emily created a more central and strangely compelling character in the threatening otherness of *Wuthering Heights'* Heathcliff, whose origins are never explained, only suggested through his dark hair and dark skin color, with this ominous description: "half-civilised ferocity lurked yet in the depressed brows and eyes full of black fire." Whatever he is and wherever he came from, Heathcliff is certainly not a normal Englishman.

Today, with the DNA analysis of ancestry.com and 23andme, Heathcliff—like the rest of us—could have his genetic makeup specified in the various percentages of multiple sources. Little is hidden. Not only is ethnic heritage pretty much of an open book today, few corners of the world have escaped filming, their landscape, architecture, and inhabitants uploaded to YouTube. And when they experience some manner of newsworthy upheaval, it's available on cable in real time.

We're no longer able to discuss those others as simple and laughable in their remoteness from atomic bombs or their desperate desire to learn how to rumba. Certain commercials do still promise sunny pleasures on white sand beaches where smiling people of color pamper vacationers with food and drink, although increasingly some of the pampered paying guests are turning out to be themselves people of color.

But now for many the reaction to the other is fear of threats, the ferocious black fire of dark-skinned people—Islamic suicide bombers, Chinese hackers, Donald Trump's rants of invasion across the Mexican border by

Hispanic rapists, sex slavers, and M13 murderers. "Make America Great Again" translates as "Make America White Again." If you can't find an attic large enough to lock away all those dangerous foreigners, lock them out by building a wall.

Bongo Bongo Bongo, keep 'em in the Congo, keep 'em in Iraq, keep 'em in Nicaragua. Any place but where I ahm.

Sources

"Civilization (Bongo, Bongo, Bongo)," 1947; written by Bob Hilliard and Carl Sigman. At least five recorded versions have made the *Billboard* magazine charts—those by The Andrews Sisters and Danny Kaye, by Louis Prima, by "Smilin'" Jack Smith, by Ray McKinley, and by Woody Herman.

"The Coffee Song," 1946; written by Bob Hilliard and Dick Miles, first recorded by Frank Sinatra.

"The Maharajah of Madagor," 1948; written by John Jacob Loeb, Lewis Harris, recorded by Vaughn Monroe and Ziggy Talent.

"Managua, Nicaragua," 1946; written by Irving Fields, the lyrics by Albert Gamse; the recording by Freddy Martin and His Orchestra reached the *Billboard* best-seller chart on January 31, 1947 and lasted eleven weeks on that chart, peaking at #1.

"Rum and Coca Cola," 1945; written by Lionel Belasco with lyrics by Lord Invader. The song was copyrighted in the United States by entertainer Morey Amsterdam and became a hit in 1945 for the Andrews Sisters, spending ten weeks at the top the *Billboard* Pop Singles chart.

Knowing Your Father: DNA and Identity

"It is a wise child who knows its own father."
—Homer, *The Odyssey*

Several women I know were stunned in later life by the discovery that the man they had long considered to be their father was not the man whose sperm actually fertilized their mother's egg. Their pasts—all that they had taken for granted about their personal histories—suffered an upheaval, lifelong assumptions thrown into chaos, with a bombardment of new facts to explore and shape. Memories, experiences, assumptions became confused shards, any attempts to piece them together undermined by large chasms of ignorance.

In one case, the woman discovered through a long-withheld admission that her origin was the result of her mother's one-night stand with a stranger. In another involving a close friend, the discovery emerged after weeks of pondering the results of an ancestry.com DNA analysis. My friend's brother, two years younger, had mailed his sample first, just curious. His report came back that he was 43% Jewish and 50% Polish.

Perplexed, my friend agreed to be tested too, with a very similar result. She and her brother had always believed their families on both sides to be Roman Catholics who had originally emigrated from Poland. How could this be an accurate finding? The results also linked them to a young man in California. Through online detective work that included census data and a newspaper archive, she discovered that her biological father was the Jewish insurance salesman who had visited frequently to collect payments. The fact that he fathered two children clearly meant a long-term affair with her mother, not a drunken interlude. Eventually, my friend learned his name and even saw a photograph of him. The emotional result was even more confusion and upset.

Heritage Erased: Dani Shapiro

The writer Dani Shapiro, in her mid-fifties, experienced a similar shock, but with an opposite ethnic surprise. All her life she had considered herself to be the daughter of a man called Paul Shapiro and a member of a prominent Orthodox Jewish family whose lineage went back for many generations on her father's side. In fact, according to DNA analysis, she was only half Jewish, the people she had considered extended family for more than fifty years now questionable in their relationship, the culture that had immersed her only partly hers. Blonde, pale, and blue-eyed, she was used to being told, you don't look Jewish, and now she knew why. Rather from emigrating from an Eastern European shtetl, her paternal ancestors had arrived in North America around the time of the Mayflower.

When Shapiro finally accepted the DNA evidence, she was devastated. She describes the reaction in her book *Inheritance*:

I woke up one morning and life was as I had always

known it to be. There were certain things I thought I could count on. I looked at my hand, for example, and I knew it was my hand. My foot was my foot. My face, my face. My history, my history. After all, it's impossible to know the future, but we can be reasonably sure about the past. By the time I went to bed that night, my entire history—the life I had lived—had crumbled beneath me, like the buried ruins of an ancient forgotten city.

Before her son's bar mitzvah, she had taken care to instill to him his heritage: "It felt urgently important to me, to make Jacob aware of his ancestral lineage, the patch of earth from which he sprang, the source of a spirit passed down, a connection." Yet now she had lost a fundamental answer to the question, "Who am I?" Who was she and where did she belong?

She writes: "Philosophers, who love nothing more than to argue with one another, do seem to agree that a continued, uninterrupted sense of self, 'the indivisible thing which I call myself,' is necessarily implied in a consciousness of our own identity."

Existential Uprooting

For good or ill, even when tensions and alienations are deep, most people need to live with the conviction of being a member of an extended family and, in particular, being the child of a certain mom and a certain dad. That's where they came from, with all the biological, cultural, and historical baggage they carry through our lives. Even if they rebel against that heritage, they have a clear center, a distinct point of departure.

But what if those essential assumptions are suddenly wiped out after a spit into a test tube or a discovered document or an uttered revelation?

From an existentialist perspective—the assumption that we are thrown into Being—we seek the foundation of an identity, something with which to authenticate ourselves—roots. That term can be taken in its cultural connotation as well as its botanical metaphor—tentacles that position us in a firm ground. Dani Shapiro and the others were uprooted by a categorical discovery. After the shock, they were compelled to plant themselves into fresh soil and endure the bewilderment of a new cultural environment.

Beyond the personal, the existential dilemma broadens into a theological dimension. The philosopher-critic Stanley Cavell explores these implications in the introduction of his study, *Disowning Knowledge: In Seven Plays of Shakespeare*. A follower of Cartesian skepticism, he interprets those plays from that perspective, explaining, ". . . what I have called the truth of skepticism, that the human habitation of the world is not assured in what philosophy calls knowledge."

Therefore, if knowledge—what we consider to be solidly factual—is undermined, we lose assurance of our place in the world, our existence. If the knowledge of our father is discredited, our lives—to use Shapiro's word—"crumble" through the loss of connection to something substantial outside ourselves. Cavell puts it this way:

> A metaphysically desperate degree of private bonding, of the wish to become undispossessable, would seem

> to be an effort to overcome the sense of the individu-
> al human being not only as now doubtful in his pos-
> sessions, as though unconvinced that anything really
> belongs to him, but doubtful at the same time whether
> there is any place to which he really belongs.

We don't know where we belong and have to start from scratch to discover something to hold onto and affirm our identity.

Parental Divinity

Much more often than not, when we are young children, reaching the state of cogency, we consider our parents to be god-like figures who know and control, beings who will nurture and guide us, whom we can turn to for comfort when in distress. If not exactly worship, we regard parents with a kind of reverence. Even when we come to know their limitations, flaws, and failures, for most of us vestiges of that early-stage relationship linger at our core.

Jean Piaget, in *Child's Conception of the World*, posits that "The child in extreme youth is driven to endow its parents with all of those attributes which theological doctrines assign to their divinities—sanctity, supreme power, omniscience, eternity, and even ubiquity."

Cavell considers our notions of God as an antidote to skepticism, a basis of a kind of certainly that allows us to feel at home in the universe: "In Cartesian episte-mology God assures the general matching of the world with human ideas of it by preserving it, its matching and its existence; in Lockean society God assures our general human claims to possession and dominion of the world by having given it to us." This notion of a divinity who created a world that embraces human needs offers great comfort. Disbelief threatens psychic upheaval.

That's why emerging doubts about parental powers can undermine the child's entire existence. Piaget cites his colleague Pierre Bovet's quotation of Edmund Gosse's reaction when Gosse first heard his father say something he knew was not true:

> Here was the appalling discovery, never suspected before, that my Father was not as God, and did not know everything. The shock was not caused by any suspicion that he was not telling the truth but by the awful proof that he was not as I had supposed omniscient.

As a result, the loss of God or the certainty of God is a source of great doubt about our place in the world and our connection with everything that is outside us. Cavell writes:

> But Descartes's very clarity about the necessity of God's assurance in establishing a rough adequation or collaboration between our everyday judgments and the world (however the matter may stand in natural science) means that if assurance in God will be shaken, the ground of the everyday is thereby shaken.

If Gosse considers his father's flaw an appalling discovery, how much worse to learn that the man you had always considered to be your father was, in fact, not the man who had given you life and a firm place in the scheme of things.

Even if Shapiro did not consider her father a deity, she enjoyed years of devotion to him and to his memory after he was killed in a car crash. When a DNA test, shattered her assurance in his paternity, her everyday crumbled. Cavell reached such a conclusion about the vulnerability of the everyday through a philosophy of skepticism, Shapiro—like my friend—through a personal crisis that obliterated long-believed knowledge.

Discovering the Biological Father

My now half-Jewish friend knows little more of her deceased biological father than a name, a photograph, and some few details of his life and work. She still has not come to terms with her origins. Fortunately for Shapiro, she was able to know and meet the man who had donated his sperm as a young medical student, now a retired physician she calls "Ben Walden." They communicated and interacted personally, coming to like one another, Shapiro even befriending his daughter, her biological half-sister.

Shapiro, in her search, enjoyed many advantages the vast majority of people lack. She is a prominent writer, married to a successful journalist and filmmaker with exceptional research skills, connected to many people who can offer information and strategies, in possession of the credentials that allow her to gain access to physicians and theologians. She is successful and appealing. Privileged. "Ben Walden" and others in his family read several of her books. Clearly, she is a daughter any man could be proud of.

Yet her many attributes, as much as they helped Shapiro cope, did not shield her from the traumas of her origins. They did not answer the existential question of, Who am I? Really?

Never Knowing the Biological Father

Literally knowing her biological father makes Shapiro unique in comparison to the thousands of humans conceived through artificial insemination unlikely to ever know. Many, however, are trying. Today breaking anonymity and revealing the identify of sperm donors has become a complex legal, ethical, and medical issue, exacerbated by the emergence of DNA testing and the resistance of donors and sperm banks.

But beyond those aware of the mystery of their biological origins, there may be many thousands more who will never know the man they assume to be their father is not the man who engendered them.

Steve Olsen, whose article titled "Who's Your Daddy?" that appeared in *The Atlantic*, suggests, "Widespread genetic testing could reveal many uncomfortable details about what went on in our parents' and grandparents' bedrooms."

Speculation on how many people don't know their real father varies. Olsen writes, "In graduate school, genetics students typically are taught that 5 to 15 percent of the men on birth certificates are not the biological fathers of their children." Russ Kirk, in a 2011 online posting, cites biologist Robin Barker, who reports in his book *Sperm Ward: The Science of Sex* that the percentage of surprise fathers ranges according to geography and economic status: "Actual figures range from 1 percent in high-status areas of the United States and Switzerland, to 5 to 6 percent for moderate-status males in the United States and Great Britain, to 10 to 30 percent for lower-status males in the United States, Great Britain and France."

Embracing Uncertainty

While fortunate to be aware of both her social and biological fathers, Shapiro still struggled with questions of identity. Ultimately, she turns to the philosophical as an antidote to the psychological, ironically embracing a version of Cavell's skepticism as the best solution to her dilemma.

She tells of receiving in an email from her biological half-sister a passage from the work of Pema Chödrön, a Buddhist teacher and writer. "To be fully alive, fully human, and completely awake is to be continually thrown out of the nest. To live fully is to be always in no-man's-land." These words come as yet another revelation, an answer that makes her particular dilemma just one extreme manifestation of the general human condition.

> I had felt every day since the previous June that I now lived—exiled, forever wandering—in no-man's-land. But the truth was that this had always been the case. Any thought of solid ground was nothing more than an illusion—not only for me but for all of us. Those words: Completely awake. Live fully, sent to me by the half-sister I had never known. I had strived for those states of being all my life, while a part of me slumbered. We will

have been like dreamers. Now there would be no more
slumber. You will be set free.

Days later, recalling Keats' notion of negative capability and the embracing of uncertainty, she experiences a further insight. "In this direction lay freedom, and,
paradoxically, self-knowledge. By my being willing not
to know thoroughly who I am and where I come from,
the rigid structures surrounding my identity might
begin to give way, leaving behind a sense of openness
and possibility."

Many of the decisions people must constantly make
through the days of their existence disturb the comfort
of the nest, forcing them to live in a no-man's-land of
ephemeral existence while they crave the certainty of an
essence.

Most of those distraught over the uncertainties of
their origin, however, lack Shapiro's intellectual and
emotional resources, terrified by the prospect of openness rather than embracing it. They are desperate to
know their fathers and all the comforting certainties
they want to believe that entails.

My friend, while not as accepting of her circumstances as Shapiro, has—I believe—overcome the initial shock of the revelation. Possessing her own creative
intelligence, after seeking more information about her
biological ancestry, she has moved on, recognizing that
she has become the person she is regardless of the sperm
that engendered her. Yet, despite that degree of certainty,
the deception gnaws.

Sources

Stanley Cavell. *Disowning Knowledge: In Seven Plays of Shakespeare*. Cambridge University Press, 2003.

Steve Olsen. "Who's Your Daddy?" *The Atlantic*. July-August 2007.

Jean Piaget. *Child's Conception of the World*. trans. Joan and Andrew Tomlinson. Routledge & Kegan Paul, 1967.

Dani Shapiro. *Inheritance: A Memoir of Genealogy, Paternity, and Love*. Alfred A. Knopf, 2019.

Grieving

FOR SEVERAL WEEKS AFTER MY WIFE, Alison, died—amid the time-blurring burdens of informing friends, making arrangements, and notifying bureaucracies—I spent a good part of the day sitting in a chair and staring into space, tethered by a sense of absence. If I could make myself get up, what would I do, where would I go? Eventually, I had to feed myself or the cats or check the mail—more sympathy cards and the paperwork of mortality. Then back into a chair. Was this grief or just being stunned by the forever change in my circumstances? Or was there a real distinction between those alternatives? And, if I was grieving, was it for Alison or for myself?

My pondering of grief has been accentuated through my participation in a weekly Zoom group. Hearing what obsesses the others allows me to relate my own emotions to theirs. Some seem traumatized even after a year or more since the shock of death. A few people report being emotionally numb, unable to interact with friends and family. Several are upset because no one close to them seems to understand the state of their grief. In contrast, I deliberately reach out to seek the company of others and immerse in people, music, and videos to divert myself. It's an unsatisfactory evasion.

Initially, I felt a form of survivor's guilt; for example, when I took a walk in the park while aware that such an experience would have given Alison great pleasure and that my own previous enjoyment had come from sharing the walk with her. Why had I been the one to live and be there, reminded of her satisfaction when she never would again?

I believe I'm past that stage. Now, when I do things or go places she really enjoyed, I like to believe that I'm sharing a vicarious happening. But is that a ruse to avoid an immediacy of grief?

In truth, grief can come upon me suddenly when I think I'm immersed in an activity that has nothing to do with my loss. Suddenly, I see a photograph of Alison or an object she treasured, and tears flood my eyes. I miss her. A mutual friend called it "a sense of emptiness," and I ask myself if that is the essence of grief, a state I should acknowledge and accept as inevitable.

But is that what grief is really about? What are people actually grieving? At times, I think it's a form of self-pity for having to exist with that emptiness, a disorientation from the forced imperative to reconstruct my life and develop new ways of being. After forty years, sharing a life with Alison had become a very comfortable norm. We existed in an ongoing present while sharing memories of the past. No other person could ever fill that role, could exchange in the shorthand of a relationship that came from being in the same places at the same time, that could unleash a richness of common memories with just a phrase.

I still remember details, but the fullness of what happened is limited by my aloneness, partial and incomplete. And, of course, new memories will never be created for the future. Existing alone lies at the heart of the emptiness. Her presence enriched the day with shared reminders.

I've also wondered about proximity and grief. Over those forty years, except for a couple hundred days out of thousands, Alison and I were together continuously. I've lost friends and siblings but do not grieve for them nearly as intensely. I believe that is because they lived their lives elsewhere, in another context, no matter how emotionally close we were. While I miss them, they were not essential to my daily living. In fact, we went though most days apart.

With Alison that wasn't true. While we may have been in separate places for hours at a time, we came together at the beginning and end of each day, discussing those hours apart, giving those hours more meaning through the sharing. Unlike others I was with only occasionally, for Alison I am constantly reminded of her absence, that I can no longer walk into another room and find her there. Yet, I intentionally have left her clothes in closets and dresser drawers, her wallet and reading glasses on a nightstand as if she were still around to use them.

So far, all I've come up with as a source of grieving is what I've lost because Alison is dead. But part of me, less specifically, is aware of what she has lost. She did not fight dying because she knew from early in her diagnosis that she had no hope and, at the end, chose palliative care over further treatment. She knew it was useless to rage against "the dying of the light". She accepted it rationally and calmly. For her the process took only a few months, which is fortunate because she would not have wanted a long decline and suffering.

Still, I'm frequently aware of occasions and people and events around me that she would have greatly enjoyed, that would have elicited her special laugh. There's so much she has been deprived of, that would have given me pleasure in watching her experience. It's her loss of the ability to encounter another happy memory.

But in truth, that's just a rationalization. Ultimately, in grieving for all that Alison is missing, I'm seeking an excuse to keep her with me because my life is so much less without her, doubly aware of what is no longer possible.

Yet, grief is also the price of love, of caring so much for another person that her removal from my life becomes a source of great emotional pain. As much as the loss hurts, it's worth it for the richness her presence brought over many years.

Outliving Society's Capacity to Care

DESPITE THE RAPIDLY GROWING NUMBER of aged in America, the ranks of geriatricians are not keeping up with the needs for old people's medical care. So reports the *New York Times*.

According to projections based on census data, by the year 2030, roughly 31 million Americans will be older than 75, the largest such population in American history. There are about 7,000 geriatricians in practice today in the United States. The American Geriatrics Society estimates that to meet the demand, medical schools would have to train at least 6,250 additional geriatricians between now and 2030, or about 450 more a year than the current rate.

Unfortunately, geriatrics is the least popular of all specialties for internal medicine residents. Even though it requires another year or two of training, the annual income averages $20,000 a year less than that of a general internal medicine practitioner and half that of a cardiac surgeon.

Because of this disjunction between the growing numbers of people living longer and longer and the increasing lack of specialists to address their unique needs, our society faces an escalating dilemma. Better drugs, earlier interventions, more exercise, and healthier diets are increasing life spans for large numbers. The fortunate spend those added years with minor issues and pass on relatively quickly; the unfortunate require ongoing medical attention, lingering in a state of compromised health. But the fact that more and more Americans refuse to shuffle off before they get really old places multiple burdens on the system, especially given the shortage of people willing to attend to the aged.

Beyond having an intellectual curiosity about this troubling prospect, as one of the aged, I am also part of the problem because I've survived so long. The *Times* article appeared shortly before my eightieth birthday, a cautionary predictor of my future if I end up with serious health-care needs. I have been further warned—and more openly—by recent visits to and news of age-mates, signs of the medical declines of people I've known for decades. They—we—overload the schedules of doctors, nurses, and caretakers, not to mention the nation's healthcare budget. The Centers for Medicare & Medicaid Services reported in December 2015: "Per person personal health care spending for the 65 and older population was $18,424 in 2010, 5 times higher than spending per child ($3,628) and 3 times spending per working-age person ($6,125.)"

The mind fades, organs malfunction, joints creak, bones snap, the body breaks down. Here's some anecdotal evidence. Recently I received the latest report about a man in his nineties who is in a Florida rehab facility with a leaky heart valve and congestive heart failure. Not long after, at another rehab center, I visited a friend my age receiving therapy after burn surgery. It was lunchtime, and we sat in a dining room with her 97-year-old roommate, as people in wheelchairs, including a former governor, rolled past to their tables. Others on foot maneuvered with canes and walkers. A few shuffled unaided but seemed about to topple over.

Two days after my rehab visit, I drove into New York City with a 90-year-old friend to have lunch with another person, in his mid-eighties, who had suffered a stroke a while ago. He has some short-term memory and mobility issues but a good command of the past, and he can hold a lively conversation. But he requires therapy and someone to drive him. Another friend from my undergraduate years called to tell me that his wife, whom I've known almost as long, had been diagnosed with Alzheimer's. She is sleeping much of the time and asking the same questions again and again. They are seeking a residential facility.

Then there are the cancer victims, primarily women friends who have had breast cancers, mastectomies, radiation, and chemotherapies; lymph nodes excised; temporary baldness. For a number of men I know, the less fatal and less complicated equivalent has been prostate cancer.

Many of my aged acquaintances have, like me, survived serious health problems, such as heart attacks, serious fractures, joint replacements, malignancies, and surgeries, conditions that at one time would have been quickly fatal. Even the healthiest of the aged tend to forget names or where they left their keys or reading glasses or why they walked into a room. Gawking at shelves, they block supermarket aisles. They dawdle when driving. It's no wonder that the young think, mutter, or shout out loud—Get out of the way, old man (or lady)!

To paraphrase Yeats, this is no country for old men and women, and yet we oldsters hang on to existence.

And, despite our aches, pains, and physical and mental limitations, a good number of us enjoy dining, traveling, listening, viewing, and, when our eyesight permits, reading.

But what's the incentive for doctoring the elderly—people whose ailments are inevitable, whose visits provide less income, who groan and complain, who often expect medical miracles and are resentful at the failure of physicians to perform them? As Americans, we—young and old—expect every problem to be fixable, whether it's conflict in the Middle East, the loss of manufacturing jobs, destructive storms, or a malfunctioning heart. Decrepitude is defeat, and something should be done about it.

It is no wonder fresh med school graduates picking a residency specialty choose one that earns more, offers more prestige, less stress, and usually leads to feel-good results like Lasik-improved vision and wrinkle-free skin. Dermatology has become the field of choice for young physicians. According to one study, "while both dermatologists and geriatricians spend a minimum of 4 years in postgraduate training, geriatricians earn less than half of a dermatologist's income."

Still, geriatricians bring in a median annual income of just under $200,000, many times more than that of the workers engaged in hours of hands-on involvement with the sick and aged. Many elderly people depend on the daily care they receive from caretakers employed in assisted living, nursing homes, or home care. For little pay and constant pressure, these healthcare workers dress, feed, bathe, and change diapers. Some of their patients are dead weight, others abusive, still others delirious.

As the population ages, and especially as the number of Alzheimer's and other dementia cases grows, the need for such caretakers is booming. The Bureau of Labor Statistics has estimated that by 2022 the United States will need 48 percent more—1.3 million—home nursing and personal assistants. Beyond the handful that serve willingly—for example, helping aging relatives—the majority of such workers fall into the profession as a job of last resort, often reluctantly. They would be ecstatic to be geriatricians, who, after a day of seeing patients, are able to go home to an affluent life away from old people.

The caretakers are often immigrants or African-Americans, and are paid as little as $10 an hour, and on average just over $20,000 a year. Their work is demanding, often unpleasant, often frustrating. According to Alana Semuels in *The Atlantic*, "One in four live in households whose income is below the federal poverty line . . . Unsurprisingly, the field has a high turnover rate—some estimates put it as high as 60 percent." One in three elder-care workers do not themselves have health insurance, either because of employers not offering it or because the workers cannot afford the premiums.

It's a Catch-22. The medical community fixes many once-fatal problems and extends life expectancy, and this puts more pressure on physicians, nurses, and those in the trenches, such as caretakers, as well as on children of the aging, who may also end up giving a lot of time and money to their parents' care.

As I enter my ninth decade, I'm functioning pretty well for my years, still working out in the gym, traveling, teaching, reading, writing, cleaning litter boxes, closing in on the post-op five years that will make me an official cancer survivor. But my remaining years most likely can be counted on my fingers—perhaps of one hand, less likely of two. Something—a burst artery, a cell gone berserk—is bound to go awry in not too long. If I'm lucky it will be a swift process. I will quickly become one less burden for the gerontologists and the overworked, if even available, health aides. Otherwise, I may find myself one of those whose lingering, unhappy lives are occasionally interrupted by visits from more mobile friends, by drip-feedings, by being turned regularly to prevent bedsores. I'd have a title but not the wherewithal to produce an essay called "Longevity and Its Discontents."

Sources

Katie Hafner. "As Population Ages, Where Are the Geriatricians?" *New York Times*, January 25, 2016.

Kathryn Joyce. "Home Care in Crisis." *In These Times*, October 9, 2014.

Karen E. Lasser, Steffie Woolhandler, and David U. Himmelstein. "Sources of U.S. Physician Income: The Contribution of Government Payments to the Specialist-Generalist Income Gap." *Journal of General Internal Medicine* 23(9), September, 2008: 1477–81. Source of comparison of dermatologists' and geriatricians' incomes.

"NHE [National Health Expenditure] Fact Sheet." *The Centers for Medicare & Medicaid Services*, December 3, 2015.

Alana Semuels. "Who Will Care for America's Seniors." *The Atlantic*, April 27, 2015.

Energy Flow and Healing

In the 1960s, people spoke of good vibes and bad vibes as metaphors for the moods of social interactions. The vibes, in effect, were emotional signals a person gives out through body language. For example, happy, smiling people were thought to have positive effects on those around them. That is, good vibes. In contrast, grumpy, morose people send out bad vibes that bring others down. In one sense, the terms were just a matter of giving a name to the obvious. Happiness or unhappiness in a person can be infectious.

But it turns out that the nature of these so-called vibes is much more complex, often not visually apparent and not limited to the effects on other people. We can send ourselves good and bad vibes too. In the half-century since the nineteen sixties, research has revealed that a form of vibes actually exists within us and around us and that we all possess the ability to use them for healing ourselves and others.

This tangible energy can be demonstrated right before our eyes. That's exactly what Jean Marie Rosone did when I was present. She is the coordinator of Oncology Integrative Medicine at Atlantic Health, which has recognized the strengths of complementary medicine techniques throughout its hospital system. Atlantic Health is hardly alone in applying the benefits of these techniques, which are used in most of the country's leading hospitals.

Atlantic Health employs such integrative therapies as meditation, stress reduction, guided imagery, yoga, Jin Shin Jyutsu, reflexology, Reiki, acupuncture, massage Healing Touch, Therapeutic Touch, Music Therapy, Art Therapy, and Sound Healing.

Using pairs of people and one blindfolded volunteer, Jean Marie showed how thoughts can dramatically produce dramatic physical effects on our muscular strengths and weaknesses. First, she had two people stand beside each other, one holding out an arm and the other trying to push it down. In the initial test, one person said his or her real first name. The arm held strong. But when the person spoke a false first name, the arm gave way.

That result might be dismissed with the explanation that both people were aware of what was true and what was not. But in the next test, the person holding out the arm had both unspoken true and false thoughts that the pusher had no way of knowing. Here again, true meant the arm could not be pushed down; false meant it could.

A more complex test involved the blindfolded volunteer standing in front of the group to demonstrate that our thoughts can affect another person, not just ourselves. When Jean Marie gave a thumbs-up signal, those in the group were directed to have positive thoughts about the volunteer; thumbs down meant negative thoughts. Every time Jean Marie gave the thumbs-up sign, she could not push down the volunteer's arm. But with each thumbs-down she could.

Beyond accomplishing an impressive revelation, Jean Marie was revealing a larger, more important point about the powers of our thoughts and other forms of energy most people don't consider.

Research has shown that an upbeat attitude can stimulate our own healing. A study conducted by Johns Hopkins Medicine concluded that "People with a family history of heart disease who also had a positive outlook were one-third less likely to have a heart attack or other cardiovascular event within five to 25 years than those with a more negative outlook."

Quoted in *Scientific American*, science journalist Jo Marchant reports, "There are now several lines of research suggesting that our mental perception of the world constantly informs and guides our immune system in a way that makes us better able to respond to future threats."

And it's not just thoughts. For example, touching or just the energy from our hands can provide a healing benefit. Atlantic Health's integrative medicine includes Energy Healing Modalities in which therapists place their hands on or near a patient's body with the purpose of consciously directing or modulating the individual's energies through interactions with the therapist's energy field. The goal is stimulating the body's own natural healing.

Jean Marie had the group prove to themselves that each one can apply his or her own hands to relieve stresses in specific parts of the body by moving a hand over the troubled area and releasing self-energy to ease the problem, such as moving a hand over the bowels for digestive issues.

These demonstrations served as an introduction to the wide range of healing possibilities available to integrative medicine specialists and to each one of us in our own homes.

Kinesiology

Many of the energy techniques included in integrative therapies can be grouped under the larger category of kinesiology. First developed in the 1960s with the discovery that each muscle in the human body is related to an energy circuit and each circuit is connected to an organ. Since then, many different branches of kinesiology have evolved with the aim of restoring balance to three key areas of health—structure (muscular-skeletal), mental/emotional (psyche), and biochemical (nutrition).

As a holistic therapy, kinesiology looks beyond the condition of the physical body itself to include the environment and the psychological state of each individual. Because kinesiology considers the body's overall state of structural, chemical, and emotional balance, it is capable of addressing a wide range of health issues. These may include stress; allergies and food sensitivities; nervous disorders; muscle, bone and joint pain; headaches; hormonal imbalances; fatigue; insomnia; and emotional issues and learning difficulties.

If the body is under stress from causes such as trauma or nutritional deficiencies, it will block energy flow within the body. This stress in the central nervous system is reflected in specific muscle patterns. Kinesiology treatment is designed to clear blockages by stimulating the body's innate healing capacity to allow it to resume normal function.

Initially skeptical of the notion that "that your subconscious can talk via your muscles," psychologist Susan

Heitler, PhD, writing in *Psychology Today*, experienced a complete reversal of her opinion. After observing how kinesiology sessions actually led to people overcoming PTSD and emotional pain like anger, anxiety, depression, Heitler is now convinced that "everyone's subconscious brain has capacities for guiding healing that go way beyond what we normally give the brain, or the muscles that speak for it, credit for."

The same technique of muscle testing arm strength or weakness Jean Marie demonstrated at the group meeting is used in kinesiology to reveal energy blockages when the practitioner light-touches acupressure points on the body that relate to glands and organs. If that aspect of the body does not suffer a blockage, the arm cannot be moved. If it is blocked, the arm drops with the slight pressure. The blockage can manifest in a physical symptom such as a sore throat or headache or a matter of emotional stress.

Once a blockage is identified, an individual possesses the capability for self-correction by touching a specific point on the body. Of course, the person must be taught where to touch to relieve a certain blockage.

Kinesiologists emphasize that their approach is not meant to be a substitute for traditional medicine. People still should have an appropriate blood tests, X-rays, or other diagnostic analyses. And kinesiology will not cure major illnesses such as cancer, diabetes, or heart issues. The techniques will, however, provide assistance in coping with the physical and emotional consequences of major health problems, and it can be used to relieve or lessen the effects of less critical issues such as headaches, fatigue, and stress.

In the United States and Canada, 471 universities offer bachelor's degrees in kinesiology, with doctoral degrees available in 45.

Despite the number practitioners, most people in the U.S. and the world have no idea of the potential within them.

The Sources of Morality

Review of *The Atheist and the Bobobo* by Frans de Waal (W. W. Norton, 2013)

PRIMATOLOGIST FRANS DE WAAL in his book *The Atheist and the Bonobo* uses bonobos to take on God, or more precisely those people who are convinced moral standards would not exist without the authority of a Supreme Being. From that perspective, morality is an attribute limited to the human realm, essential to our unique and special status in the eyes of one's Creator, a set of tests for the judgment that will determine our eternal status in the afterlife. For de Waal, that's counterfactual thinking. From his long career of observing primates, bonobos among them, he finds a form of moral behavior innate to their interactions with others of their kind, similar to that of all mammals and possibly even other animal species. Such animal morality predates that of humans, and what humans exhibit—or hope to exhibit—shares the same roots. According to de Waal, moral codes aren't dictates of divinity but rather manifestations of inborn compassion that existed before human religion.

To epitomize the belief he is denying—the conviction that people require the imposition of rules from a divine source—de Waal refers to a statement attributed to Ivan, the atheist of Dostoevsky's three Karamazov siblings. In de Waal's version it is, "If there is no God, I am free to rape my neighbor!" Most people quote Ivan as saying, "If God does not exist, then everything is permitted." It turns out that those words are also inaccurate. What Ivan said in the novel (as translated from the Russian in the Pevear-Volokhonsky English version) is, "Without God and the future life? It means everything is permitted now, one can do anything." Although the familiar and inaccurate condensed version may imply the necessity of a deity to control human wantonness, the inclusion of "the future life" actually completes the argument: if people didn't have the threat of eternal punishment hanging over them—along with the corollary reward of eternal bliss—they would have no incentive to behave morally, no reason to restrain their innate tendency to run amok with unrestrained license.

For many in the secular West, including those who would read de Waal's book, he may be restating the obvious in denying a divine basis for moral codes. Yet Ivan's proposition in its various iterations resonates for billions of people who have never read *The Brothers Karamazov* and perhaps don't even know such a novel exists. Those billions believe humanity needs the presence of an omnipotent and omniscient punisher and the promises of a rewarder.

The Pew Findings

A 2014 Pew survey reveals a geographic set of responses to the notion of God as requisite for morality, and national or regional clusters of believers. This study of 40 countries produced dramatic differences according to continent and region. Great majorities in Africa and the Middle East consider a deity necessary for moral behavior, as do 99 percent in certain Asian countries. Europe overall goes in the opposite direction, but the U.S. is split. Of course, some are skeptical about the validity of such surveys. Still, despite the American exception, one conclusion might be that the more affluent and technologically advanced a country, the less likely its citizens are to believe they need a deity to make them behave, and another, that the Pew people are onto a wide global split in beliefs about the relationship of God and morality.

Contrary to the religious believers, de Waal argues that divinity has nothing to do with morality. In the book, he presents evidence to build a case that if God does not exist, everything is not permitted to bonobos or chimpanzees or, for that matter, kittens and puppies. More accurately, they do not permit themselves everything.

Tooth and Claw

Some in the secular world who find de Waal's dissociation of a deity and morality old news might consider his view of the natural world more problematic. They make a fundamental distinction between the human and animal realms, with immoral animals indulging their vicious predatory appetites, supported by the poetry of Alfred, Lord Tennyson, the Pulitzer Prize winning essays of Annie Dillard, and the fiction of Joseph Conrad. Although he does not refer to these writers by name, de Waal in his observations of animal interactions mounts an argument against assumptions such as theirs.

Tennyson famously claims a fundamental opposition between Nature and God's love in Canto 56 of *In*

Memoriam:

> Who trusted God was love indeed
> And love Creation's final law
> Tho' Nature, red in tooth and claw
> With ravine, shriek'd against his creed

Here the poet echoes the Great Chain of Being theory, where humans exist in a unique realm. As St. Augustine puts it, "Man is an intermediate being, but intermediate between beasts and angels. A beast is irrational and mortal, while an angel is rational and immortal. Man is intermediate, inferior to the angels, and superior to the beasts." While literal acceptance of that theory may have faded, belief in the unique status of humans has dominated for millennia. Descartes considered animals essentially automata unable to feel pain, and most have followed his lead, at least in assuming that animals don't deserve the moral consideration reserved for humans because they are "other."

Annie Dillard, in *The Pilgrim at Tinker Creek*, through her close observation of the creatures she encounters during her Thoreau-like retreat to nature in western Virginia, describes the teeming fecundity, waste, and death she finds all around her. She sees evolution as the source of these destructive excesses, and her findings could be considered a detailed case against the claimants of intelligent design. Multitudes of living creatures, from the microscopic on up, are lost along the way, while only a fraction survive. "It's a hell of a way to run a universe," she writes.

Dillard essentially separates humanity from the natural realm where "[e]volution loves death more than it loves you or me." Nature values the individual being "not a whit," while humans value the individual "supremely." In the context of the Great Chain of Being, she might find such valuing an angelic attribute far apart from those irrational doomed beasts. For Dillard, the distinction is stark:

> But wait, you say, there is no right and wrong in nature; right and wrong is a human concept. Precisely: we are moral creatures, then, in an amoral world. The universe that suckled us is a monster that does not care if we live or die—does not care if it itself grinds to a halt. It is fixed and blind, a robot programmed to kill. We are free and seeing; we can only try to outwit it at every turn to save our skins.

In *Heart of Darkness*, Joseph Conrad dramatizes the lure of the bestial. As Conrad's narrator Marlow illustrates through the story of Mr. Kurtz, who started off as the ideal of European civilization and ended up a head-hunting barbarian, the irrationality of the beasts is the stronger force, pulling us downward, requiring a great effort to resist. "The horror! The horror!"

Marlow tells of Mr. Kurtz to three other seasoned seafarers on a yawl moored on London's Thames at twilight, where a speaker cites the achievements resulting from the many voyages that began from the river. Marlow puts those triumphs into perspective: "And this also . . . has been one of the dark places of the earth." "We live in the flicker," he adds, implying that such light—enlightenment—is easily extinguished as we revert to the brutality lurking at the heart of us.

Not so, says de Waal. Not so in any way. He cites

findings that hearts of most species are not dark at all. He would judge Marlow's claim a version of Veneer Theory, a once-dominant biological belief that morality is just a thin surface concealing the entirely selfish nature of creatures, including humans. That theory, de Waal asserts, has recently been disproven by "overwhelming evidence for innate empathy, altruism, and cooperation in humans and other animals." He cites neuroimaging evidence that we have "biases toward cooperation," our brains activate positively when we assist others.

In fact, de Waal might be considered to be reversing The Great Chain of Being, with our—human—better sides not the result of angelic emulation but rather rooted in the altruistic inclinations of so-called beasts.

According to de Waal, moral systems are basically structures of social codes supported by two re-enforcers—from within, empathy and good relations with others to avoid trouble, and from without, the threat of penalties by higher-ups. For de Waal, that doesn't mean a deity capable of meting out eternal damnation. Bonobo actions emanate primarily from within much more than from the threat of punishment, although bad behavior can be prevented by watchful eyes or, if it occurs, disciplined by authority figures.

Boost and Share

For de Waal the word for such cooperation is "compassion," and he finds that quality in animals demonstrated daily. He cites examples of younger chimpanzees supporting an arthritic old female by bringing her water from a source and boosting her to climb to a higher level, as well as evidence of smaller primates sharing food rather than fighting over it. As a result, he considers that "Contrary to the customary blood-soaked view of nature, animals are not devoid of tendencies that we morally approve of, which to me suggests that morality is not as much of a human innovation as we like to think." Instead of tooth and claw, it's often boost and share.

Noting paleontological findings that Neanderthals cared for afflicted individuals, he considers this information evidence of a communitarian heritage that "suggests that morality predates current civilizations and religions by at least a hundred millennia." De Waal documents animal empathy to prove mammals give and want affection, perhaps because most mammals spend their early days with mothers who nurture their young. He does recognize that birds exhibit similar characteristics of caring and loyalty, also asking if some reptiles can be placed in the same category.

He tells of an exchange he had with the Dalai Lama, who wondered if animals as a whole, in doing all they can for themselves and their progeny, reveal that "all life is caring" and that "compassion goes to the root of what life is all about."

Other researchers have discovered what they consider altruism in acts such as bees dying for the hive or slime mold cells cohering into a single organism to allow reproduction. But de Waal makes a distinction between such behavior and mammalian empathy, calling what bees and slime mold do a "preprogrammed tendency to sacrifice oneself for the genetic good": "Mammals have what I call an 'altruistic impulse' in that they respond to signs of distress in others and feel an urge to improve their situation."

Although de Waal cites behavioral examples of many animal species, both his own observations and those of other researchers, bonobo relationships are central to his conclusions. Dutch born and educated, his first extended research was conducted in the chimpanzee colony at the Arnhem, Netherlands, zoo, resulting in his first book, *Chimpanzee Politics*. Since then he has written more than a dozen additional books as well as many articles, focusing on primate social behavior and conflict resolution. He now teaches at Emery University.

The existence of bonobos, despite their large and distinctive size, is a relatively recent discovery, a phenomenon of 1929 when both German and American scientists realized the creatures weren't a subset of chimpanzees but an entirely different species, with unique anatomy, much closer to humans than any other ape. In an earlier book, *Bonobo: The Forgotten Ape*, de Waal discussed these primates in detail. In this recent book he uses examples of their behavior to support his position on compassion.

Bonobo Social Life

Bonobos differ significantly from chimps when it comes of aggression and conflict. Chimps will kill one another over territory. Bonobos, while initially hostile to neighbors by shouting and chasing, soon calm to engage in sexual activities with the strangers, actualizing the hippie mantra of the 1960s to make love, not war. De Waal quotes the Japanese primatologist Takeshi Furuichi: "With bonobos everything is peaceful. When I see bonobos they seem to be enjoying their lives."

An obvious question arises. Are bonobos unique from other creatures in their inclinations? Or are they more benign examples of mammalian compassion, just far less prone to mixing in violence? While de Waal finds bonobos unusual in their blatant sexuality, he puts them on a continuum with chimps and humans. While the three species share many characteristics, a number are geared to each species and would be inappropriate if emulated fully by the others, such as casual bonobo public sex for people. He calls humans "bipolar apes," as domineering and violent as chimps on bad days, as nice as bonobos on good.

Assuming that de Waal is right about the similarities between human and bonobo compassion and empathy, those similarities must be considered with a basic question: are animal emotions only similar to ours in some respects, or do they reveal evidence of a meaningful morality?

Future Lives

Beyond that question lies one more fundamental. Remember, the full English version of what Ivan Karamazov said includes "the future life." Assuming that a life beyond this one exists, is it limited to human beings, alone of all living things in possession of a soul? And if a life beyond this one is the ultimate hope of humanity, can morality be merely a way station, a divine test that must be passed to earn a future in a state of perfect harmony, where such a thing as morality is no longer necessary?

Animals, even those as highly evolved as bonobos, don't seem to have to pass such tests. In fact, they don't appear to ponder, debate, and anguish over moral choices as humans often do. Their acts of compassion may be innate emotional responses. Consider a cat that climbs on the lap of an ailing human to purr comfort and an hour or so later pounces on a mouse to snap its neck. Humans, if the count of *YouTube* hits is any measure, can spend hours watching videos of kitten cuteness, then use that same computer to cheat on their income tax or log off to commit adultery with a neighbor's spouse. The mouse-killing cat is just doing what comes naturally, without an instant of a qualm. The humans, the guilt varying with their degree of callousness, do know they are violating a rule.

The Range of Consequences

Of course, in the human realm, the ramifications of a specific action can be widespread, debilitating to hundreds and thousands of individuals and perhaps whole areas of the globe. We struggle with the question of whether it's moral to send a drone to kill a single terrorist planning an attack that will kill hundreds, perhaps thousands. The worst a malevolent bonobo can do is kill another bonobo or two. And a bonobo would just act in an emotional outburst without all that preliminary mental baggage.

But are human choices a difference of degree or kind? Is it just the advances of technology that give humans the capabilities of drones, missiles, chemical poisons, nuclear devices, and other weapons that extend the range of pain and destruction far beyond the damage done by our prehistoric ancestors' sticks and rocks? Would a furious bonobo push the button if it had access to such a button?

What often gives humans moral quandaries is the matter of consequences. In many cases, when a behavioral decision is more than an automatic response, we ponder what that decision means. If the question involves sending a drone to kill a terrorist, one immediate conundrum involves our right to take another human life based on the possibility that act will save many others. Some may consider such a choice a political or social dilemma and the decision a result of a cost-benefit analysis. Whether the problem is moral, social, or political, an act of contemplation is involved. Would a bonobo have the capacity or inclination to weigh such a moral choice or make such an analysis?

Kant's Imperative

One thinker who says no is Emmanuel Kant of the categorical imperative, the theory that human morality is the result of our higher reason, absolute and unconditional, what we must do without an ulterior motive, such as the attainment of eternal bliss or avoidance of prison or eternal damnation. He distinguishes between rational beings, who are ends in themselves not to be used as means by others, and non-rational beings, who are things that may be used as means. In *Lectures on Anthropology* he elucidates further:

> The fact that the human being can have the representation "I" raises him infinitely above all the other beings on earth. By this he is a person ... that is, a being altogether different in rank and dignity from things, such

as irrational animals, with which one may deal and dispose at one's discretion.

Kant qualified what he means by discretion, noting an obligation to relate kindly to animals ethically, but not because of what they are; rather, brutality to animals suggests cruelty to other humans.

De Waal, from his understanding of animals, dismisses Kant. He calls Kant's elevation of "pure reason"—the notion that a true morality exists for human minds to discover—"an odd idea." "The idea that morality can be argued from first principles," he says, "is a creationist myth, and a poorly supported one at that." Despite its complexity, moral law "doesn't imply a logical design," and de Waal finds no convincing argument exists to make that case.

Fundamentally, de Waal does not put humans and animals—bonobos—in such extremely disparate categories. A bonobo is an "I" just as much as any human, de Waal or you or me.

Bottom-up Morality

We know animals, at least those higher up the chain, can suffer forms of post-traumatic grief—the great ape who sees its mother killed, the elephant mourning in the graveyard of its species, the dog grieving for its master. But do they feel remorse and guilt, brooding for years over an act of questionable morality inflicted on another person or even a pet? Do animals crave forgiveness? Charles Darwin proposed six universal emotions shared by humans and animals (anger, happiness, sadness, disgust, fear, and surprise). We have seen that animals are capable of compassion. Researchers aren't sure about guilt. But de Waal tells of a bonobo named Lody, who in a moment of panic bit off the finger of a veterinarian and immediately slunk off in remorse. When the vet returned fifteen years later, according to de Waal, Lody remembered and approached her, eager to see the hand he had bitten, an indication that bonobos care about relationships and possibly forgiveness.

Unlike the billions throughout the world, according to Pew, who find a powerful god a requirement as a source of morality, de Waal sees matters the other way around: humans need a concept of a god to help enforce morality, "to help us live the way we felt we ought to." Even though de Waal is not a religious believer, he denies the stance of the contemporary militant atheists. Humans, he says, benefit from the communal connections of religion. That pragmatic justification, of course, would hardly satisfy the billions whose faith is crucial to their existence.

He calls his understanding of morality a bottom-up view:

> The moral law is not imposed from above or derived from well-reasoned principles; rather, it arises from ingrained values that have been there since the beginning of time. The most fundamental one derives from the survival value of group life. The desire to belong, to get along, to love and be loved, prompts us to do everything in our power to stay on good terms with those on whom we depend.

Still, are human moral systems just an evolutionary advance on those of elephants, chimps, and bonobos?

Rather than requiring a deity to tell people what's morally right, do all those billions posit one to provide absolute authority for the behaviors they already value and the choices they make?

So what is permitted? That's not a question a bonobo would ask. Bonobos possess an innate guidance system, just doing what comes naturally, usually something sexually pleasurable. Still, de Waal asserts that such actions are not without restraints because of group expectations and controls on conduct. All is not permitted:

> Even if he [a bonobo] lacks notions of right and wrong that transcend his personal situation, his values are not altogether different from those underlying human morality. He, too, strives to fit in, obeys social rules, empathizes with others, amends broken relationships, and objects to unfair arrangements. We may not wish to call it morality, but his behavior isn't free of prescriptions either.

Humans also live by rules of guidance, often codified by ecclesiastical, legal, political, or cultural bodies. People, for the most part, know in advance the learned acceptable behaviors of their societies. At heart, those codes may only be systematized elaborations of the compassion other mammals have shown since there were mammals, and perhaps long before that.

Eating Intelligent Beings

A review of:

Animals and Society: An Introduction to Human-Animal Studies by Margo DeMello (Columbia University Press, 2012)

Animal Rights Without Liberation: Applied Ethics and Human Obligations by Alasdair Cochrane (Columbia University Press, 2012)

Without Offending Humans: A Critique of Animal Rights by Élisabeth de Fontenay (University of Minnesota Press, 2012)

MANY STUDIES IN RECENT YEARS have demonstrated that animals—from mammals to birds and insects—possess much greater intelligence, problem-solving ability, and sensitivity than previously assumed. This new knowledge has led to reconsiderations of the interactions between human and nonhuman animals, specifically theories of how humans should treat other creatures, including the question of animal rights.

The three books discussed here address these issues, agreeing the relationship of humans and other animals is much more complicated than simply that of master and resource. The authors view nonhuman animals as complex beings deserving benevolent consideration, arguing for better treatment than now exists. Where they disagree is on the fundamental question of whether humans have the right to slaughter creatures for food, despite the fact that these creatures should possess certain basic rights. But if animals are denied the right not to be killed to satisfy human dietary cravings, do any other rights matter?

For centuries the great majority of humans have considered animals inferior others and taken them for granted as resources, existing to serve our needs, including dietary. Aristotle argued animals had no interests of their own and lacked reason, relegating them to positions far below humans on The Great Chain of Being. More crucial for recent centuries has been Descartes's mechanistic separation of humans and animals, which considers the nonhuman lacking souls, minds, or reason and, therefore, not deserving of rights. Writing about animal consciousness in the essay "One of Us" in the *Lapham Quarterly*, John Jeremiah Sullivan notes that Descartes considered animals mere automata, paraphrasing: "We look at them—they seem so full of depth, so like us, but it's an illusion. Everything they do can be attached by causal chain to some process, some natural event." Because animals lack mental capacity that provides for awareness, Descartes wrote, animals do not feel "pain in the strict sense."

Even though other thinkers of Descartes's time, like Hobbes, Voltaire, and Spinoza, disagreed with the automata conclusion, finding evidence for some manner of consciousness, they still did not deny human power over animals, Spinoza stating that any argument against slaughtering animals is not based on "sound reason." For him, animal nature is not like ours.

Although Darwin initiated the study of animal consciousness in a lab setting, it was, as Sullivan notes, the many experiments beginning in the twentieth century that have significantly deepened human understanding of animals, for example, the evidence that dolphins grieve, that bees communicate through a dance code, that birds recognize themselves in mirrors. He cites the conclusions of the recent document, "The Cambridge Declaration on Consciousness in Nonhuman Animals," which states, "Humans are not unique in possessing the neurological substrates that generate consciousness."

More and more research reveals evidence of greater animal intelligence and sensitivities than our predecessors imagined. In a *Wall Street Journal* essay titled "The Brains of the Animal Kingdom," primatologist Frans de Waal cites studies that demonstrate such intelligence, noting, "A growing body of evidence shows, however, that we have grossly underestimated both the scope and the scale of animal intelligence. Can an octopus use tools? Do chimpanzees have a sense of fairness? Can birds guess what others know? Do rats feel empathy for their friends? Just a few decades ago we would have answered 'no' to all such questions. Now we're not so sure."

Previous tests to determine animal IQ, de Waal argues, have been deficient, biased against the animals because of anthropomorphic misassumptions. For example, because chimpanzees failed at recognizing photos of human faces, they were judged deficient. But when an experimenter thought to show them photos of chimp faces, they were expert at knowing who was whom and even which offspring belonged with which mothers.

Elephants were considered unable to recognize themselves in a mirror until experimenters realized the mirrors used were too small to produce a full reflection. Another error led to a conclusion that elephants could not use tools, in this case a stick, to retrieve food because the elephants were expected to use their trunks to guide the stick. But the stick blocked their acute sense of smell and, thus, their ability to detect food. Instead, given a different implement, an elephant was able to push with its feet a box to stand on in order to reach something edible.

Other experiments proved that rats confronted with a trapped companion and a chocolate container did not hog the treat, but rather freed the other rat first and then shared the chocolate. De Waal concludes, "[S]cience keeps chipping away at the wall that separates us from the other animals. We have moved from viewing animals as instinct-driven stimulus-response machines to seeing them as sophisticated decision makers."

How should this knowledge of intelligence and awareness affect the ways humans regard nonhuman animals and relate to them? If animals can engage in creative thinking and can demonstrate caring, how should humans develop guidelines for interacting with them?

Not that we treat other human beings all that well, as any history text or half-hour of cable news makes clear. Yet we have standards that we are supposed to apply—The Golden Rule, the Universal Declaration of Human Rights. Should there be a declaration of universal animal rights to help us define the nature of our obligations to nonhuman creatures? And how should we balance human rights with animal rights? Most crucially, does our desire to consume meat override that of animals not to be slaughtered and eaten?

The French philosopher Élisabeth de Fontenay addresses these issues in *Without Offending Humans: A Critique of Animal Rights*, translated into English by Will Bishop. The title reveals her concern as she examines a range of ethical and philosophical writings to determine how humans should behave toward animals and what to do if calls for animal rights conflict with the rights of humans.

De Fontenay is hardly insensitive to the abuse of animals and the need for protections. She speaks of "the mysterious responsibility of good will toward beasts," but does not consider these beasts deserving of equal consideration because they lack "certain singularities of human reality." While criticizing the philosophical anthropocentrism of the post-Cartesian tradition, she believes that we will never be able to avoid a minimal amount of such anthropocentrism.

Her most vehement attacks against radical animal sympathizers are directed toward the utilitarian positions of Peter Singer and Paola Cavalieri. Singer, she says, argues for an egalitarianism that applies to both humans and animals and goes to the extreme of considering people with extreme cognitive limitations more appropriate candidates for vivisection than animals and places fetuses and newborns in a category with reptiles and fish, below that of certain mammals. Cavalieri, she says, claims that the "intellectually disabled human" does not deserve a higher moral status than a great ape.

The positions of Edmund Husserl and Maurice Merleau-Ponty meet de Fontenay's approval because, she says, they are the only Western authors who "account for animals ontologically" and propose the case that the treatment of animals should be based on the fact that "they have worlds, worlds that can intersect with the world of men." These worlds of animals possess their own integrity and should be appreciated, but they do not belong in the same realm as the world of men [i.e., humans], to be regarded with the exact same ethical guidelines. While animals should have rights, they are not the same rights as those possessed by humans.

But de Fontenay also criticizes Husserl because he establishes a "troubling analogy between the more evolved animals and the insufficiently watchful man," ignoring the beasts' lack of a rational aim, of the *cogito*, and theoretical thinking. As in her much more severe condemnation of Singer and Cavalieri, she reveals a basic objection to equating humans and animals.

Her recognition of animal worlds does not really solve the question of hierarchy. Even though they may prove to have interests and demonstrate reason, what does that mean to the chain of being if they are not elevated to a level equal to that of humans? When our worlds intersect, should the human always prevail, giving us priority to slaughter and eat, cage for experimentation, dislocate from habitat for developments that house and feed humans? De Fontenay does want limits on our human powers over animals.

Her concluding chapter, "The Ordinariness of Barbarity," makes a passionate argument that even though animals and humans do not exist at the same level, the world is afflicted by a widespread cruelty toward beasts:

> For as things currently stand, it is no longer only death that constitutes the most atrocious violation for an ani-

mal, but the enclosure of its poor body and its poor life in the terrifying abstraction of the pet store and the laboratory or in the concentration-like space of factory farming.

All this occurs not because of sadism but rather of indifference. "Our model of industrialization of the living is fundamentally nihilistic." Humans have a duty to develop legal reforms that regard the status of animals with a sense of kinship and pity. Yet her arguments put limits on how much kinship and how much pity. The right not to be abused on the farm does not extend to denial of the abattoir, rather that humans should practice benevolent slaughter.

Because de Fontenay's work is a collection of essays, the book is not a systematic approach to the questions of animal rights. Such a method may be found in Alasdair Cochrane's *Animal Rights Without Liberation: Applied Ethics and Human Obligation*. His work can be considered a model of lucidity. He explains his premises, the sources of his reasoning, the strengths and weaknesses of other theories on the subject, and the implications of his conclusions when applied to specific areas of human-animal interaction.

His title, however, sets up a straw man, the notion of total liberation as developed by Tom Regan, whose argument demands, in Regan's words, "the total dissolution of the animal industry as we know it." Cochrane dismisses what he concludes would be animal liberation in the early pages of his book and turns to considering a theory of animal rights emerging from systematic moral reasoning and principles. Such rights do not preclude the continuing existence of various forms of an animal industry, as long as the animals within those domains are not subjected to unnecessary pain and suffering.

For Cochrane, animals do not wish to be free because they lack the conception of such liberty. They are, for example, quite content to live in a home as pets as long as they are not abused or mistreated. Humans are under no imperative to liberate them. "So while sentient animals have particular interests that impose strict duties on us in a whole variety of contexts, those duties do not include having to refrain from using, keeping, and owning them."

He calls his an "interest-based rights approach" in that sentient animals possess interests. Such interests, however, are not absolute; they vary with context. In each context the interests of animals must be identified, evaluated, weighed against any competing interests, and balanced against the burdens they place on those with responsibility for them.

Cochrane's approach amounts to a pragmatic set of principles to be applied when humans interact with animals in a range of specific situations—animal experimentation, agriculture, genetic engineering, entertainment, environmental obligations, and use in religious practices. He writes separate chapters on each area and comes to a similar conclusion in each case. We have a moral obligation not to kill or inflict pain. In practice, that means forbidding animal sacrifice, sterilizing rather than hunting to control species overpopulation and damage to the environment, and experimenting without killing or hurting. Fundamental to Cochrane's conclusions is his belief that animals have a right not to be killed.

Many people would agree with certain of his conclusions, for example, those opposed to inflicting pain on and killing laboratory animals or to herd-thinning hunting seasons. However, Cochrane's ultimate position on animals in agriculture—consistent as it is with the logic of his overall position—faces widespread lack of support because of its implications for the great majority of humans. A good number will be disturbed by his descriptions of the sufferings inflicted on animals in factory farms, and some people will be willing to pay higher prices for free-range meat. Nonetheless, most people will object to Cochrane's arguing, on the basis of animals' rights not to be killed, for eliminating meat from the human diet, even if steers, pigs, or lambs lived free-range lives before being trucked off to the slaughterhouse, even a "humane" one of the sort designed by animal behaiorist Temple Grandin. Despite the nutritional studies supporting Cochrane's claim that we can survive well as vegetarians and even benefit from avoiding meat, the reality is that people will refuse to give up steaks and Big Macs and that people in countries emerging from poverty associate meat eating with a reward of growing affluence.

With likely reactions to the case against meat, the moral argument for animal rights confronts a practical barrier that can undermine its less controversial aspects. If we can kill a beast in order to enjoy its flesh charbroiled, why shouldn't we kill lab animals if their deaths will result in a new medication that reduces human suffering and mortality? We've back to the chain of being that makes our human welfare more important than that of animals.

A broader perspective on the complexities of human-animal relationships and animal rights may be found in Margo DeMello's *Animals and Society: An Introduction to Human-Animal Studies.* Ostensibly a textbook for a beginning course in a new academic discipline—HAS (Human-Animal Studies)—DeMello's book surpasses the typical textbook in offering a well-written overview of the field, with historical and cultural coverage of the changing categorizations of animals, the social construction of animals, the various human uses of animals, attitudes toward animals, and symbolic manifestations of animals.

Citing criticisms of calling the discipline human-animal studies, as if humans weren't animals, DeMello offers a more accurate definition of the field: "the study of the interactions and relationships between human and nonhuman animals." She also places works like those of de Fontenay and Cochrane in the field of critical animal studies (CAS), which she says is "dedicated to the abolition of animal exploitation, oppression, and domination." CAS has a clear political and moral agenda, while HAS attempts to provide a contextual understanding of how humans regard for and treatment of animals developed and changed.

The question of flesh-eating provides a good example of the distinction. Rather than addressing the moral validity of cultivating creatures to kill and eat in just the present, she goes back to the Paleolithic Era for the history of what served as food. Our pre-human ancestors probably had diets like today's chimpanzees, mainly vegetarian with some supplementation by a hunted or scavenged small animal. As the stone tools and arrow-heads of those times reveal, as humanoids evolved and brains became larger, they formed societies of big-game hunters. Overhunting depleted some animal populations and led to different meat sources, such as small animals, birds, and fish. Therefore, twenty-first century humans descend from thousands of years of meat-eating ancestors. A CAS proponent like Cochrane probably would say that by now, as have our hunting and agribusiness skills, our moral capacities should have advanced to the point of realizing the meat eating is wrong.

DeMello devotes a chapter to the question "The Making and Consumption of Meat." There she considers meat taboos, how animals become meat, meat consumption in the past, modern meat production, why we eat meat, slaughterhouse workers, cultural implications of producing and consuming meat, and the ethics of meat eating. While Cochrane came to his conclusions from an exclusively moral analysis, DeMello considers the ethical just one variable of approaching humans as carnivores.

Yet her approach also builds a case against meat eating, or at least against the consumption of meat produced through the abuses of factory farming, in which animals are considered products rather than sentient beings. Though a short recapitulation of the relationship of Americans to meat, she argues that such farming is not "natural," primarily because of recent customs and cultural assumptions, which, lately, have been bolstered by agribusiness advertising and government subsidies.

Now most of us take for granted that a daily meal or two with meat is the way it's supposed to be, but DeMello stresses that this is a relatively new expectation for Americans and for most of the world. In the United States the abundance of undeveloped land for grazing coupled with the coming of the railroad and, later, refrigerated cars permitted the large-scale raising of livestock and the distribution of its results throughout the land. Meat can be produced cheaply in this country. While throughout much of modern history, meat eating was associated with status and power and often limited to a small elite, everyone now has access to tons of beef, pork, and chicken.

Yet humans do not need meat to survive. They just think they do. And not only do animals on factory farms suffer lives that are nasty, brutish, and short, so do the humans who work in slaughterhouses to butcher them for delivery to markets. These workers are exploited by their bosses, paid minimally, and often injured or made ill from viruses and bacteria in the buildings. Annual turnover is almost one hundred percent.

While raising meat on open grazing land was ecologically sound, factory farms cause great environmental harm as a result of the 1.5 billion annual tons of waste and the amount of water used. Moreover, the more meat people consume, the greater the increase in worldwide human hunger for people who could survive on the grain used to fatten animals or on the grain that could have been grown on land being used to raise livestock. In addition, current studies have shown a correlation of eating red and processed meat with colon cancer.

Despite the case she builds, DeMello, unlike Cochrane, does not argue that animals have a right not to be killed. Her pragmatic analysis, ultimately, might lead to a denial of using animals for food. But she does not go there. Opposed to the cruelty of factory farms, she wants better treatment of animals, and she applauds the growing numbers of vegetarian alternatives and people who are eating free-range eggs and animals raised locally under "humane" conditions; that is, non-factory farming. With this stance, she agrees with de Fontenay, who calls for "kinship and pity" in our relationship with animals.

Cochrane, of course, would argue that a "humane" death is still a form of being killed and, therefore, a violation of animal rights. DeMello notes that animals raised for food are not given names the way we do our pets because "We do not eat those with whom we have a personal relationship." Is this distinction between pets and food just a rationalization? In some parts of the world, as DeMello points out, dogs are raised for the dinner table.

The recent outrage at the discovery of horsemeat in some mixtures labeled as beef demonstrates all people might draw a line or make distinctions, refusing to eat certain kinds of meat, but for some people horsemeat is on the far side of the line. People in one culture are often disgusted by what members of a rival culture eat, often using such food as a term of derision, e.g., the English have called the French "frogs." Yet few cultures, if any, don't kill some nonhuman animal to satisfy their dietary preferences.

It may be that other animals, like other people, have a right not to be killed. Yet such a right will continue to be idealistic as humans continue to slaughter their fellow creatures for food, just as they continue to slaughter other humans for territory and resources, or because of religious beliefs, tribal hatreds, or just sadism. Some people may brood over the horrors of factory farming, as they sit at the dinner table taking a knife and fork to a leg of lamb or a porterhouse steak taken from humanely raised creatures.

Personally, I am convinced by Cochrane's logic. Before reading him, I would have been satisfied by the similar positions of de Fontenay and DeMello. I was already buying range-free chickens, imagining happy creatures pecking away at grain with the run of the farmyard, unlike the factory-farmed fowls with severed beaks and flesh pumped with hormones. But now I cannot deny that after a few months of good times the range-free hen is still killed and hacked apart so I can devour a drumstick or a slice of white meat. And that's not to speak of cattle, pigs, and sheep. Although they're not common in suburban New Jersey, I have hiked among them in European fields and enjoyed their company, even made eye contact. I'd never consider butchering any one of them for a meal, and I don't have to. I can survive without being a carnivore. Life is the ultimate right for both human and nonhuman animals. To conclude less is a rationalization.

Seeking Creatural Diversity

A review of *Polymorphous Domesticities: Pets, Bodies, and Desire in Four Modern Writers*, by Juliana Schiesari (University of California Press, 2012)

MY FRIEND, THE POET RENÉE ASHLEY, a consummate dog lover, displays a sticker on the back of her car with a canine paw print and the words, "Who Saved Who?" It should be "Whom," but no matter. The message might have served as an epigram for Juliana Schiesari's study, which challenges the hierarchical assumptions of "speciesism." Unfortunately, in the works of three of the four writers Schiesari considers—Edith Wharton, Djuna Barnes, and Colette—the animals are interpreted as manifestations of human drives, symbols rather than creatures with their own integrity. Only J.K. Ackerley's dog exists as a distinctly independent being that can legitimately raise the question of who saved whom that can help us try to transcend our limited human perspective and appreciate the otherness of other beings.

In her previous book, *Beasts and Beauties: Animals, Gender and Domestication in the Italian Renaissance*, Schiesari connected the "new" (as of the Renaissance) phenomenon of domesticated animals (pets) with a new concept of the home, which became, she wrote, "a uniquely private enclosure, where the *pater familias* rules over his secluded world of domesticated wife, children, servants—and animals." *Polymorphous Domesticities* continues her exploration of the subject, but, as a result, her attack on paternalistic domination undermines what could have been a real consideration of the connections between humans and animals.

Most writers who create animal characters turn them into playthings or symbols and in that way "use" them. Schiersari claims that she wishes to "deconstruct the binary animal/human divide."

Schiersari's introduction appears to promise such a study. Rather than the scientific approach to fathom animal behavior sought by many behaviorists and biologists, she argues instead that what must be understood is "the relation between humans and animals." Rejecting the extreme anthropomorphism that leads people to dress pets in baby clothes and subject them to other forms of cuteness, Schiesari calls for a "self-reflexive" anthropomorphism that acknowledges both the similarities and differences between humans and animals, allowing each species its uniqueness, as the "only epistemologically viable way we have of understanding animals." Such an approach allows us to connect with animals intellectually and emotionally. Schiersari argues that if we fail to acknowledge the similarities between humans and animals, as well as the differences that give them their distinctiveness, we are in danger of objectifying them as objects of repression and even death and destruction.

But having said this, she falls back to the subject of human power relationships, such as paternalism. She finds the assertion of "primacy and superiority of humans over all other creatures" as the ground of "humanist" thought, resulting in a fundamental "speciesism," and as "the model for the development of various intra-species claims to hierarchy, including racism, sexism, classism, and other forms of institutionalized ideologies of privilege and 'normativity'." Her condemnation of humanism as a source of subjugating animals may go back to its Renaissance origins and its contemporaneous appearance with the *pater familias*. Perhaps she is echoing Edmund Burke's criticism of humanism as the deification of man, and by implication making humans superior to animals. But dominion over the animals is asserted early in Genesis, long before the Renaissance, and tends to be the assumption of most people at most times in most places.

The shifts of emphasis in the introduction suggest that Schiesari is caught in a conflict between asking who dominates over whom and who can save whom, in the sense that animals can enlighten us, humans, about who and what we are in the scheme of things. In her brief Afterward, she states that, "Literary portrayals of polymorphous domestic relations between different beings, whether humans of the same or different sex, or nonhuman creatures, raise significant questions about the potentials inherent in these relations and challenge our received understanding of what it is to be human or animal." But most of her book fails to take up this challenge.

Living with cats, domestic short hairs, has made it impossible for me not to consider the human-animal question often; several times a day would not be unusual. My wife and I share a house with four of them—three males who are bff's and an old female who doesn't like the males and keeps to herself. It seems every time we enter a room, there's a cat sprawled on some surface. They interact with us frequently, seeking a lap on which to purr, but a cat noise from another part of the house will perk up ears and result in a leap to see what's going on. That's only fair. If the phone rings, we shift our attention to the signal from the human world.

Does that mean that we humans and cats just occupy the same space, maneuvering around each other, the cats just using us as sources of food and sites for sleep, not to mention for keeping their litter boxes clean? I don't think so. While they're cats and we're people, we don't live lives apart. Despite spending the majority of our time in our different realms, we connect often throughout the day, certainly aware of each other and sharing a need for affection. They desire closeness and touch. And they have an instinct to comfort us when my wife and I are ill or blue.

Cats snuggle and present throats for stroking, heads for butting, flanks for rubbing. Do they love us as we do them? I have no idea. What is love for a cat?

Long before reading Schiesari's introduction, I often sensed the cats were sure they understood fully what was going on in the context of their lives and that events outside this context didn't matter. But, in turn, I also sensed that we, humans, exist with the same assumption that we know what it's all about. So, it would seem that cats and humans share different versions of the same delusion.

Sociobiologist E. O. Wilson opens his essay "On the Origins of the Arts" (in the May-June 2012 issue of the *Harvard Magazine*) with an extensive litany of the limitations of human perceptions:

Our sensory world, what we can learn unaided about reality external to our bodies, is pitifully small. Our vision is limited to a tiny segment of the electromagnetic spectrum, where wave frequencies in their fullness range from gamma radiation at the upper end, downward to the ultralow frequency used in some specialized forms of communication. We see only a tiny bit in the middle of the whole, which we refer to as the "visual spectrum." [...] Of the sound frequencies all around us we hear only a few. [...] Our greatest weakness, however, is our pitifully small sense of taste and smell. Over 99 percent of all living species, from microorganisms to animals, rely on chemical senses to find their way through the environment. They have also perfected the capacity to communicate with one another with special chemicals called pheromones. In contrast, human beings, along with monkeys, apes, and birds, are among the rare life forms that are primarily audiovisual, and correspondingly weak in taste and smell.

In short, we are limited to a miniscule fraction of all around us and don't even know what we don't know because of what Schiesari might call our humanistic bias. The cats curl a lip when they enter a new smell into their huge data banks, a smell they will never forget. Do they also pity our olfactory limitations?

I wish Schiersari had focused on such matters through *Polymorphous Domesticities* and let animals be animals with their own complex integrity. As indicated by its subtitle—"Pets, Bodies, and Desire in Four Modern Writers"— the book is a work of literary study rather than a head-on critique of humanism and speciesism, or study of animal behavior, perceptions of understandings. Schiesari, at times, wants to use texts "as an important way of rethinking animal studies through postmodern theory," with a goal of "building creatural diversity." But most of her close readings focus on uses of animal characters to enact revenge on cruel and unfeeling husbands or as surrogates for the three women authors or characters to release their essential natures. Author biography is mixed with readings of the works themselves. Thus, for example, Edith Wharton's and Colette's works are read as responses to unhappy marriages to louts. Wharton's and Djuna Barnes's animals, primarily dogs, are not depicted as diverse creatures but rather as manifestations of suppressed aggressions, representing the beast within the human. These are figurative dogs.

While many literary scholars have analyzed works of literature to discuss subjects such as animal rights, sexism, imperialism, and paternalism, *Polymorphous Domesticities* blurs the case for a new approach to the relationship of humans and animals with the failings of a male-dominated society and, specifically, those of marriage in such societies. As a result, the argument for reconsidering our connection with animals is undermined.

The discussion of Wharton focuses on a single poem, "Artemis to Actaeon," and a single story, "Kerfol." In the story, "ghostly dogs wreak a Dianesque revenge upon a jealous and possessive husband who ends up dead with unexplainable canine bites all over his corpse." Barnes explores forces in female erotic relationships. "More than the mediator of desire, the beast in *Nightwood* is a powerful transformer of social, sexual, and psychical identity." The inherent animal ancestry of her character Robin is too wild to be tamed. The novel concludes with

Robin in a chapel "in beastly communion" with a dog, both woman and animal on all fours in wild dynamism, both making barking sounds until they fall together. Yet in Schiesari's analysis of the Barnes novel the dog is a figure in a human drama, existing as a manifestation of a human drive, not a depiction of essential dogness.

For Schiesari, Colette does not depict animals as forces of a "female power to inflict retribution," but to celebrate domestic diversity. Schiesari, however, emphasizes Colette's first marriage to a manipulative older husband who claimed her early writings. She says that for Colette "the animal world is the antidote to an exploitative patriarchal arrangement masquerading as love and marriage." If not retribution, animals for Colette offer a rejection of and alternative to the "savage world of men and their 'civilization'." Thus, for Colette, too, in Schiersari's reading, animals serve as figures in an ideological argument rather than being explored for what they are.

J.K. Ackerley attempts to understand animals as living creatures with emotional and erotic needs.

Again, Schiesari comes closest to achieving the goal of creatural diversity in her chapter on J.K. Ackerley, "Romancing the Beast," in which her close analysis of Ackerley's autobiographical novel, *We Think the World of You*, and of his memoir, *My Dog Tulip*, explores Ackerley's relationship with the real bitch Queenie and his attempts to understand the nature of the animal as a living creature with emotional and erotic needs. Ackerley even caters to those needs (as he understood or imagined them) with caresses and sexual stimulation. He strives to accept the dog in all her canine nature, including her fluids of heat and elimination. Rather than Ackerley training Queenie as many human owners do their dogs, it is Queenie who trains him in the way of beasts. "The wisdom imparted by animals is that of the beastliness human beings deny in themselves, thereby wreaking havoc." In this case, it seems clear who saves whom. For Ackerley, unlike for Wharton, Barnes, and Colette, the animal is the true subject, grasping its essential nature is the basic quest for the human author.

Most writers who create animal characters turn them into playthings or symbols and in that way "use" them. Hemingway can evoke the power of a lion even while pursuing it as a hunting trophy. For part of a paragraph in "The Short Happy Life of Francis Macomber," he writes from the lion's point of view:

> Macomber stepped out of the curved opening at the side of the front seat, onto the step and down onto the ground. The lion still stood looking majestically and coolly toward this object so that his eyes only showed in silhouette, bulking like some super-rhino. There was no man smell carried toward him and he watched the object, moving his great head a little from side to side. Then watching the object, not afraid, but hesitating before going down the bank to drink with such a thing opposite him, he saw a man figure detach itself from it and he turned his heavy head and swung away toward the cover of the trees as he heard a cracking crash and felt the slam of a .30-06 220-grain solid bullet that bit his flank and ripped in sudden hot scalding nausea through his stomach. He trotted, heavy, big-footed, swinging wounded full-bellied, through the trees toward the tall grass and cover, and the crash came again to go past him ripping the air apart. Then it crashed again and he felt the blow as it hit his lower ribs

and ripped on through, blood sudden hot and frothy
in his mouth, and he galloped toward the high grass
where he could crouch and not be seen and make them
bring the crashing thing close enough so he could make
a rush and get the man that held it.

But even here Hemingway only imagines what the
lion sees and feels, not its essential being.

Perhaps the writer closest to grasping animal integrity is D.H. Lawrence in works like *The Fox* and *St. Mawr.*
The fox and the horse in these works do figure in the
lives of the human characters; the force of their existence
has a profound effect on the humans. But Lawrence possesses a unique ability to dramatize powers beyond the
human and to reveal how those powers transcend our
limited perspective.

As one of the characters says, "There's a terrible mystery St. Mawr," and the horse evokes disturbing realms
humans cannot comprehend:

> But now, as if that mysterious fire of the horse's body
> had split some rock in her, she went home and hid her-
> self in her room, and just cried. The wild, brilliant, alert
> head of St. Mawr seemed to look at her out of another
> world. It was as if she had had a vision, as if the walls
> of her own world had suddenly melted away, leaving
> her in a great darkness, in the midst of which the large,
> brilliant eyes of that horse looked at her with demon-
> ish question, while his naked ears stood up like dag-
> gers from the naked lines of his inhuman head, and his
> great body glowed red with power.

What humans know of the world around them, in
E.O. Wilson's words, is "pitifully small." In this context,

perhaps even expanding the knowledge of our domesticities is too limited. The cats we live among are certainly no St. Mawrs, tamed, circling their dishes at the rattle of Purina box or pop of Friskies can. No demonic red power in our suburban felines. But, despite their dependency, they are clearly other; they are not symbols, not merely manifestations of our human needs. It's a subject worthy of investigation. Perhaps one Schiesari will engage in her next book.

The Groups We Belong To

Review of *The Big Picture: America in Panorama*, from the collection of Josh Sapan (New York: Princeton Architectural Press, 2013)

THE BIG PICTURE: AMERICA IN PANORAMA celebrates both the possibilities of the panoramic camera and the manner in which the United States organized itself during the decades of the late nineteenth and early twentieth centuries. The people pictured are arranged in wide-angle spreads, layered in rows, some standing, some kneeling, some seated, most in their best clothing, assembled for an occasion important enough to be memorialized by a camera. Their groups gathered represent an extensive variety of occupations, professions, and causes, as well as others just there for a single event—associations of a particular time and place, many long-forgotten.

The unusual dimensions of this hardcover book—fifteen inches wide and seven inches high—make it difficult to fit onto a library shelf. But that shape is necessary for the great majority of the black and white prints displayed, a few so wide they take up a thirty-inch double-page spread.

Today, a hundred years after most of these pictures were taken, what could we substitute for a wide-angle photograph? Facebook friends? LinkedIn contacts? Consider the logistical impossibility of gathering those people in one place. Today's alternative might be a screenshot of all one's friends and links, but with each face in a separate box rather than a unified image.

The photographs in *The Big Picture* come from the collection of Josh Sapan, accumulated during a thirty-five-year quest. In his foreword, Sapan, president and chief executive of AMC Networks, notes, "Over time, I began to understand the odd window that the groups provided into the history of the United States." He finds that, despite the apparent stiffness of the scenes, a closer look at the expressions of the people "often reveals much in the nuance: pride, determination, focus."

Luc Sante's introduction provides information about the history, development, and uses of the panoramic camera. Celebrities such as Yogi Berra, Dick Cavett, Arianna Huffington, Norman Lear, Anna Quindlen, and Lawrence Summers contribute brief commentaries about some of the photographs. Behind the scenes for much of the text was the writer Bill Mesce, Jr.

In suits, hats, and overcoats, members of the American Iron and Steel Institute gathered in Cleveland on October 23, 1915 to inspect the ore docks. Similarly dressed but just for socialization, the men of the District of Columbia Bar to Bench attended their annual shad bake at Chesapeake Beach, Maryland, on May 13, 1916. Women are interspersed with the men in 1916 in front of Philadelphia's Convention Hall for the Associated Advertising Clubs of the World. Boston hosted the centenary meeting of the American Board of Commissioners for Foreign Missions between October 11 and 14, 1910.

Other groups pictured in the book are the National American Woman Suffrage Association; attendees at the Mohonk Peace Conference; the twenty-third annual conference of the National Association for the Advancement of Colored People (see below); a contrasting Ku Klux Klan convention, a sea of white hoods shaped like dunce caps. The Survivors of the Lawrence Massacre present a collective of a very different sort. An example of a more transitory group may be found in the 1935 photo of Inter-City Beauties performing at Showmen's Variety Jubilee at Atlantic City's Steel Pier. So many people gathered for so many different reasons, but all captured in panoramic display, the individual choosing to be a member of a posed crowd and, apparently, happy to be there.

Looking at the unusually oblong group photos assembled in *The Big Picture*, I can't help recalling a similar picture taken at the end of my high school senior trip to Washington, DC. We were lined up several rows deep on a wide lawn while a camera panned from left to right to fit us all in. Walt Beyer, from the football team, was chosen to crouch down and outrace the camera to appear in focus at both ends. Such doubling seems to be a feature of many such high-school photos from the mid twentieth century, though I didn't spot a similar antic in any of those gathered by Sapan.

But like the photograph of my graduating class— now rolled and stored somewhere in my house—those collected in *The Big Picture* remind me how almost all of the groups we belong to are equally arbitrary. Beyond the fixed relationships of the families we are born into, all others are a matter of chance and circumstance. I grew up in a certain town in a generation of men and women whose families also happened to live there. We ended up in the same schools and assembled behind desks year after year, linked as a unit until we dispersed shortly after that Washington photo. I haven't seen those people in decades, but I recall many vividly, fixed in their 18-year-old personas.

Every group I've associated with since that time has also been the outcome of arbitrary timing. Classmates in college who happened to show up in the same years. Those I've worked with and lived among. Those in my basic training company during my six-months army experience. We bunked alphabetically—Coburn, Croft, Crusade, me. Beyond relatives, all our associations are accidental. And yet, because we belong to these arbitrary groups, because they serve as sources of vital memories, they are essential in defining us.

In so many ways these groups add ballast to our lives. We're members of the class of '57, the congregation of St. Peter's Church, the Jaycees, the Steamfitters Union, Scout Troop 35, the Oddfellows—each a partial answer to the question, Who am I?

Most of the photographs in *The Big Picture*, however, recall a world of the past, not just because they are in black and white or because the people wear outdated clothing. So many represent organizations that no longer exist or merely linger as shells of their former prominence. The company shots speak of a time when businesses thrived for generations, and those employed assumed the businesses would endure forever; in many cases, their children followed them, taking jobs in the same buildings. I recall Croft, in the basic training bunk near mine, boasting of his employment at IBM. Though he had a minor clerical role, he exuded a real pride in being a part of that enterprise. Although IBM still exists today, it's a very different company from Croft's time, its once iconic personal computer branch sold to a Chinese company, its no layoff policy based on mutual loyalty of employer and employee also gone. A great number of other corporations and businesses of twentieth century are no longer with us, made obsolete by the rush of new technologies. Now for many, if not most of us, jobs and careers are transitory. Companies don't want the burden of loyal, long-time employees. Employees assume job insecurity. We've become a society of short-timers, keeping one eye open for other opportunities, frequently moving on—or being "let go."

So many of the groups we belong to now are virtual, Internet associations offering asynchronous interactions rather than real-time presence. Even groups that gather in person are ephemeral, the cast of characters shifting continually, as if with the click of a mouse. The big picture has become the fragmented picture, scattered far beyond the range of any panoramic camera.

Afterword

All this is not to say that photographs of large groups are rarely taken today. One exception is that of survivors of the Boston Marathon bombing from the one-year anniversary of the event printed on the first page of the *New York Post* of April 16, 2014.

In one sense this is an update of the "Survivors of the Lawrence Massacre" in *The Big Picture*. That 1913 photo, taken fifty years after the attack by Quantrill's Raiders, a group of Confederate guerrillas, displays men and women arranged in orderly rows, some standing, some seated, women wearing white dresses and men white shirts and ties, if not suit jackets.

The posed formality of 1913 and the clustered casualness of 2014 reveals much about changes in America even though people are still vulnerable to attacks—a hundred raiders with guns then, two men with homemade bombs now. It's hard to imagine a fiftieth anniversary of the Marathon bombing in light of the many events sure to descend upon us in coming decades, leaving their own aftermath of survivors. How will they be pictured?

WALTER CUMMINS

Where Do Humans End?

ROBOTICS AND ARTIFICIAL INTELLIGENCE are now in the news almost every day, and at the movies and on TV. Some hi-techers believe we have entered into new relationships with our digital devices. The boundaries between Us and Them may be vanishing. If we are becoming "transhumans," is it more threat than benefit?

Captain Ahab's peg leg did provide him physical balance, but—as a reminder of his maiming by the White Whale—not mental balance. It's doubtful that any member of the Pequod's crew would have considered Ahab's wooden implement a true leg replacement. We live in a different time. Late in 2014 a college student created an operational plastic hand for a seven-year-old and did it for approximately $20 in less than twenty-four hours with a 3D printer. The boy, Holden Mora, born without a natural hand, explains his prosthetic, "So when I bend my hand in like this, it closes. When I bend it like this, it opens."

A video called "The Bionic Man," which was posted as part of the *New York Times* online *Robotica* series, demonstrates two prosthetic arms controlled by the thoughts of a man, Les Baugh, who, when a teenager, lost both of his flesh-and-blood arms in an electrical accident. His upper body ends at the shoulders. The experimental contraption, developed at John Hopkins, straps to his torso and, without incisions, engages nerve endings, allowing him to grasp objects by activating the mechanical joints through conscious mental signals.

While still learning and occasionally dropping things, his arms are functioning with a form of touch, his robotic fingers closing on objects.

Where does the boy or the man end and an external reality begin?

Are Holden's hand and these arms when worn and controlled by Les Baugh integral to them or are they foreign objects? Where does the boy or the man end and an external reality begin? The question applies not just to appendages and visibly obvious prosthetic devices.

In recent years the explosion of sophisticated technologies, including biological ones, have added complexities to the issue of what's me and what's not me. Where do I end? By asking this question, I am not exploring mystical or metaphysical matters such as the connection of my being to the One, or some form of universal consciousness. I am asking about our physical bodies as they relate to various extensions and substitutions.

Such extensions and substitutions are becoming more available, with future developments sure to yield even greater refinement. They can be fashioned from organic matter, formed from metals or plastic, or involve implantation of miniaturized computer software. Whether organic or artificial, they are not the limbs and organs we were born with, or—in Holden's case—should have been born with. Does their source make a difference in their "naturalness"?

Replacement organs are already available. Some, like Holden's hand, are products of 3D printers. Of course, a successful artificial heart has been around for decades. It is a mechanism. Alternatively, patients' stem cells have generated synthetic 3D tracheas through a bioreactor process. A number of these tracheas have been surgically implanted. Because they possess the same immunological characteristics as the host patient, they do not require immune suppressant drugs. Organs such as hearts, livers, and kidneys might emerge from similar processes.

Are our extraordinary new capacities resulting in a vastly expanded *me*, or are we on the verge of making the notion of *me* meaningless?

The use of stem cells may be considered a highly developed variation of procedures in which one part of a patient's body is given a new function from its original role. For example, a piece of a leg artery ends up in the chest after heart bypass surgery or a tendon is relocated in the elbow of a baseball pitcher through "Tommy John" surgery. In these examples, it's still material from the same person. But what of a pig heart valve that replaces a defective human heart valve? Should that valve be considered a foreign object in a different category from the repurposed artery or stem-cell trachea?

> The point of the blind man's stick has become an area of sensitivity for him, extending the scope of his touch.
> –Merleau-Ponty

Let's consider a hybrid circumstance, that of a urostomy resulting from the removal of a cancerous bladder. None of us can live without a bladder, or some semblance of one. The semblance is usually an internal surgical concoction of stents from the kidneys to a tube called an *ileal conduit*, which is fashioned from a piece of small intestine emerging near the navel as a protrusion called a stoma. So far, the system is all reconfigured flesh and tissue. But then a urethane pouch must be taped to the patient's middle with an opening for the stoma. That pouch collects a constant flow of urine for emptying through a drainage outlet. It's a lifelong situation.

The pouches are temporary, usually changed every few days. As a result, although the intestinal section for the conduit is permanent, the pouch is transitory. Is it a foreign object, or is it part of the person? Does the relationship change from the time the pouch is taken out of a box and adhered to flesh? Once on the bladderless individual, it's an essential substitution.

From one perspective, external or even internal devices could be considered separate entities even though connected or implanted to serve as integral parts of our daily functioning. From another perspective, those who rely on such devices would be incomplete without them. They allow the wearers to be themselves.

We are past questioning the essential relationship of the device to the person, according to Tamar Sharon in her 2013 work, *Human Nature in an Age of Biotechnology*. In the abstract to one of her chapters she writes:

> Radical posthumanism argues for a reflexive model of technology, in which technologies are both seen as the product of human creativity and a force that shapes human existence, i.e. technologies are determinative of human experience, though not deterministic [i.e.: a likely source rather than an inevitable one]. And methodological posthumanism introduces the key concept of technological mediation, which implies that technologies are active mediators of how humans experience the world and how humans act, transforming ourselves and the world in the process. Both approaches imply an "originary prostheticity," the idea that the human exists

in relation to and is dependent on its technologies; that the human emerges as a result of this relationship.

To support her position, Sharon quotes from Gregory Bateson's 1972 work, *Steps to an Ecology of Mind*:

> It is not communicationally meaningful to ask whether the blind man's stick or the scientist's microscope are "parts" of the men who use them. Both stick and microscope are important pathways of communication and, as such, are parts of the network in which we are interested; but no boundary line—e.g., halfway up the stick—can be relevant in a description of the topology of this network.

The example of the blind man's stick leads Sharon to refer to Maurice Merleau-Ponty's earlier discussion of such a stick. He contends (in the English translation), "The blind man's stick has ceased to be an object for him and is no longer perceived for itself: its point has become an area of sensitivity, extending the scope and active radius or touch and providing a parallel sight in the exploration of things."

Following this line of thought, Holden Mora's hand, Les Baugh's arms, and an urostomate's pouch are also incomplete objects in themselves, meaningful only in relation to their actualization through human use. If we need the device to function, it is part of us. In their use, they actualize the human.

We have come a long way from Ahab's inanimate peg leg and are probably in the early days of redefining the nature of *me*, now that the bodies of our birth continue to merge with fabricated parts and pieces in a manner that blurs and could eventually erase the distinction.

Physical supplements and replacements, whether internal or external, may belong in the same category as other devices, such as the scientist's microscope, that enhance our functioning. What of our GPSes, computers, smartphones, smart watches, Google glasses, and digital clothing? What of devices that tabulate the steps we take, the stairs we climb, the level of our blood sugar, our blood pressure, even our emotional states. Millions of people, most with their original limbs and organs, have come to rely on them as the Apples, Googles, and Microsofts of the world create and sell paraphernalia we soon find we can't live without. As our extraordinary new capacities multiply, do they result in a vastly expanded "me," or are we on the verge of making the notion of "me" meaningless?

Sources

"7-year-old gets new grip on life from 3D printer." CBS News, cbsnews.com.

Gregory Bateson. Steps to an Ecology of Mind. Chicago, University of Chicago Press, 1972.

Zackary Canepari, Drea Cooper, and Emma Cott, "The Bionic Man." New York Times, May 20, 2015, *Robotica* series. Jeremy Hsu, "3D Printing Aims to Deliver Organs on Demand." September 24, 2013. Accessed via livescience.com.

Maurice Merleau-Ponty. Phenomenology of Perception. Translated by. Colin Smith. London: Routledge & Kegan Paul, 1962.

Tamar Sharon. Human Nature in an Age of Biotechnology: The Case for Mediated Posthumanism Berlin: Springer, 2013.

Harvard Apparatus Regenerative Technology. "What Organs Have Been Regenerated?" Accessed via harvardapparatus-regen.com.

RealDolls and Other Humanoids

IN ANOTHER ESSAY I WROTE about the relationship of various prosthetic devices to the people who wear them. This time my topic is humanoids. At first glance, they may seem to be very different subjects. Prosthetics often and humanoids always, however, do share roots in robotics and artificial intelligence. But, more significantly, they question the relationships of human beings to devices that possess human characteristics. Recently, humanoids have become a particular subject of media fascination. What capabilities might such creatures possess? And should we be concerned?

The potential capabilities go beyond physical functions such as their ability to perform tasks that relieve human burdens, such as lifting heavy loads or vacuuming the carpet. In those abilities, they are similar to prosthetics that accomplish what an individual cannot, though, in the case of the humanoid, it's a matter of would prefer not to. The more troubling aspect of the potential arises from the artificial intelligence embedded in humanoid chips. If a computerized device can beat chess experts or drive cars more safely than people, what might an artificial being with a human form achieve more effectively than we can? In sci-fi the humans are often humiliated by the humanoid, if not literally destroyed. Could that really happen?

Once the creature ceases to be dependent, Its cleverness
"creates a feeling of unease in those who witness it".
—Mark Crispin Miller

Let's start by distinguishing between robots and humanoids, even though they are usually linked as variations of a basic category, such as with media professor Mark Crispin Miller's term "humanoid robots." Granted that the humanoid is essentially robotic, its physical appearance is quite different from that of a robot and, therefore, so is our potential reaction to and interaction with it. Although a robot may and often does perform human functions and may even be likeable for its animate cuteness, as with R2-D2 of *Star Wars*, the robot is clearly a manufactured object, visibly a machine.

While a robotic automaton can mimic human actions, it is still a mechanical device with a combination of gears, springs, cams, and levers, such as the sixteenth-century mechanical monk built by Juanelo Turriano for Phillip II of Spain. This fifteen-inch toy still navigates today on wheels hidden by its monk's robe and can imitate walking with artificial feet. Even its eyes, lips, and head can move to suggest prayer. The monk and similar devices amaze and amuse because they are miniature novelties more admirable for the cleverness of their makers than for their relationship to humanity.

Beyond these physical versions of a clockmaker's skills, it's only been in the computer age that life-size, far less machine-like humanoids have existed. However, the human imagination has long anticipated their coming, folklore and fiction conjuring up a variety of disturbing non-humans, such as the golem of Jewish mythology or

Victor Frankenstein's creature created from an assemblage of body parts. Note that *creature* is the term used by Mary Shelley in her novel *Frankenstein*. *Monster* comes from the movie and from the jerrybuilt look of the lumbering form in the movie. The original creature on Shelley's page evokes both fear and pity because his murderous revenge is the result of his tortured awareness of his incompleteness and of his craving to be fully human.

The movie monster—nameless in the film, but often mistakenly called by the name of its creator—is borderline robotic, given the bolts in its neck, yet it has glimmerings of emotional sensitivity. The reader of the Shelley novel, however, may experience a much greater empathy for the creature because its physical appearance is only hinted at, while its inner life is revealed. It longs to be like the rest of us but lacks some essential quality—not merely a body part, some quality unavailable and unknown to Victor Frankenstein in his laboratory. In such a lacking the creature shares the mystery of psychopathic torturers and mass murderers; humans also missing something vital.

Today's technologies can turn Victor's fictional process into a literal one that produces an actual physical manifestation. Our fascination with literary non-human likenesses suggests a longstanding anxiety about their potential powers and our limitations. The message many take away from Mary Shelley's Frankenstein is "don't mess with Mother Nature," fear of forces that science may unleash, humanoids as a recent example.

Although he does not distinguish robots from humanoids per se, Professor Miller does explain the source of our radically different reactions to, say, the mechanical monk and Frankenstein's creature. "Once the creature ceases to be dependent, its cleverness 'creates a feeling of unease in those who witness it,'" Miller writes (quoting Jasia Reichardt, who in 1968 curated a show and published a magazine special edition on Cybernetic Serendipity). Miller continues:

> [T]he phrase "clever mechanism" no longer refers to the inventor's talents, but to the thing itself, with its unnatural abilities and its will to power. Thus the ventriloquist's dummy turns monstrous once it appears to take command, as in so many films and television shows; and the full-sized autonomous robot, approaching humanity as if on equal terms, is never funny, because it seems intent on taking over absolutely, irreversibly.

"Approaching humanity" is what makes the humanoid even more threatening than demonstrably "other" mechanical robots. With Frankenstein's ungainly movie monster, we know from the start to be on our guard.

An even more disturbing fear: the possibility that evil is a dark capability within human beings; the humanoid represents the worst that lies within us.

Humanoids, in contrast, assume convincing human form and emulate human behavior. Portrayed for most of a film by actors and actresses as normal-looking people, they may morph into reptilian monsters or hideous globs of protoplasm. The ultimate betrayal may be the beautiful, seductive woman transmogrified into vicious ugliness, *La belle dame sans merci*. Such transformations can evoke two forms of fear. A being in human guise suggests that someone just like us, perhaps even someone we love, can be revealed as an evil "force," especially treacherous because of its convincing deception. Perhaps an even more disturbing fear arises from the possibility that the evil is not that of an alien presence but a manifestation of a dark capability within human beings; the humanoid represents the worst that lies within us.

The 2015 film *Ex Machina* avoids such ugliness and from the first identifies the female, Ada, as a humanoid. The movie is subtle in depicting the transformation from her robotic remnants. The plot involves a young innocent coder named Caleb who is brought into the remote domain of an eccentric techie billionaire, Nathan, ostensibly so that he can administer a "Turing test" to Ada. The test is to determine whether the machine's intellectual behavior is indistinguishable from that of a human. In the case of Ada, can she think on her own, exceeding the parameters of her coding?

Initially, despite the very human face and voice, the actress playing Ada is given visibly artificial characteristics: transparent limbs that reveal inner mechanisms. But, by the end of the film, she aces the Turing test and displays greater intelligence than the two men, assuming full human form by taking an arm, hair, and simulated flesh from other experimental humanoids. Empowered, she causes the stabbing death of Nathan and the permanent entrapment of Caleb so that she can flee into a city where no one will suspect she is not a real person. Are her actions evil, or does she just want to escape imprisonment in a research facility? The movie ends with Ada out in the world with who knows what mischief ahead. She is a projection of our fears of artificial intelligence run amok.

An apparently less threatening non-human female is RealDoll, a concept formerly limited to fiction and film, now actually existing as a life-size humanoid with all the pulchritude of an airbrushed Playboy centerfold. According to a video in *The New York Times* online *Robotica* series, "In just two years, the creator of RealDoll says he will sell a robotic version with convincing artificial intelligence, blinking eyes and a mouth that moves." She talks, too, with a voice, that, at this point, sounds something like that of a GPS. But two years of development will no doubt lead to seductive breathlessness and a phone-sex vocabulary. Still, voice will be just one aspect of RealDoll's commercial function. She is a literal sex object, multiply orificed, and perpetually willing and available, never with a headache, never needing or wishing to say "No" or "Not tonight, dear."

I'm reminded of a song from the 1940s, "Paper Doll." Unlike "a fickle-minded real live girl," the paper doll can be "my own"; she's a woman "other fellows" cannot steal. RealDoll could be substituted for that lyric. Much more substantial than paper, she is the closest simulation of an actual live female possible given the current state of technology and artificial intelligence. Now, in not many months, every home, and perhaps every man's bed, can have one. Crude blowup dolls will end up relegated to attic trunks. RealDoll may not—in the present incarnation—return embraces, but she will utter words of satisfaction. In addition, a product line called Wicked RealDoll offers a "new articulated spine, which allows for completely realistic and natural torso positioning and range of motion."

RealDoll's artificial, technological pleasures join such substitutes as concocted foods, e-friendship, and e-dating.

RealDoll may be extreme, but she (it?) serves as a symptomatic embodiment of humanoid possibility and of the potential consequences for the human relationship to the real live world, including transforming our relationships with one another. The (for some) male attitude toward women has already been revealed by the use of the "date rape" drug or induced pass-out drunkenness that results in the sexual use of an unthinking object. In not too long, women are likely to have their own humanoid alternative to sex toys. Once the Real-Doll technology is perfected, the designers may create a masculine counterpart similar to Barbie's Ken, perhaps called HunkDoll. In fact, a male RealDoll is already available, but the Web description emphasizes its "oral capacity," not another attribute.

For all her apparent similarities to a human woman, RealDoll is best explained by Jean Baudrillard's 1981 theory of simulacra:

> [T]he era of simulation is inaugurated by a liquidation of all referentials. . . . It is no longer a question of imitation, nor duplication, nor even parody. It is a question of substituting the signs of the real for the real, that is to say of an operation of deterring every real process via its operational double, a programmatic, metastable, perfectly descriptive machine that offers all the signs of the real and short-circuits all its vicissitudes.

RealDoll lacks an authentic referential beyond the conjuring of male fantasies, the perfect, perpetually compliant sex partner, all vicissitudes erased, that never actually existed. Unlike the treacherous humanoid beauties of film, RealDoll won't suddenly transmute into a gelatinous slug-like being or, Ada-like, kill and imprison. Her threat may lie in continuing to be herself, a source that causes the man who uses her to lose his own humanity for immersion in a tangible unreal. In a narrow sense, she mirrors the simulated erotic make-believe of pornography and the performing prostitute. In a wider sense, she is just one more example of the abundance of artificial pleasures mushrooming from a host of technologies, such as substituting e-friendship and e-dating for friends and romance, or substituting concocted foods for real nourishment. Perhaps the RealDoll owner would be better off amusing himself with the cams and levers of a mechanical monk or with cutting out paper dolls.

Sources

Evan Andrews. "7 Early Robots and Automatons." Accessed via history.com.

Ex Machina. Directed by Alex Garland. Universal Pictures, 2015.

Jean Baudrillard. *Simulacra and Simulation*. Translated by Sheila Faria Glaser. Ann Arbor, MI.: University of Michigan Press, 1981.

Zackary Canepari, Drea Cooper, and Emma Cott. "The Uncanny Lover." *New York Times,* June 11, 2015.

Mark Crispin Miller. "The Robot in the Western Mind." In *Boxed In: The Culture of TV*. Evanston, IL: Northwestern University Press, 1988.

Mary Shelley. *Frankenstein; or, The Modern Prometheus*. New York: Dover Publications, 1994.

Fear of Heights

THE MAGNIFICENT TREE THAT WE HAD ADMIRED for our more than twenty years in this house is now a stump after a week-long process of devastation, men with chain saws dangling from ropes in the upper reaches, the heavy thuds of dropping branches. It had been our favorite tree in the neighborhood, possibly the whole town, much taller than the others, perhaps one hundred and fifty feet high, and symmetrically ideal—an archetypal tree. Although we didn't want to watch, we couldn't help being aware of the pace of denuding, looking out to see lushness hewn, long leafless shafts. Why would anyone want to destroy such a beautiful thing?

Our neighbor had been eyeing that tree for fifteen years since the time he moved in. Now and then we had discussions of the property line and finally yielded, admitting that probably seven-eighths of the trunk existed in his yard. He won.

From the beginning we knew it would be useless to play the aesthetics card, though we did slip in praise of the tree now and then. Deaf ears. He clearly didn't like trees, wasn't moved by their grandeur. In fact, he had in his first years of residence removed a row of healthy, shorter trees from the back of his yard. Without the absorbing roots, he ended up with rainfall flooding his basement.

His apparent grudge against trees seemed to arise from complaints about leaves in his above-ground pool. We even had a brief argument when he cut down a healthy twenty-foot tree on a border that was clearly half his and half ours.

But why the grandest tree in the area? We realized that leaves weren't the real reason after his son asked us, "Aren't you worried that tree will fall on your house?" We clearly weren't, given the tree's robust health and its distance from the building. Then my wife had an illumination. Our neighbor had grown up in a suburb on what had been the flat, potato farmland of Long Island. He wasn't used to tall trees. They probably frightened him with nightmares of collapse. Living objects that loomed above him must have been sources of extreme anxiety.

Until her insight, I had never thought about such fears. Then I remembered an afternoon spent in Manhattan with a woman visiting from a European city free of tall buildings. Those skyscrapers terrified her. She kept her eyes to the pavement and avoided looking up.

It wasn't until several years later that I learned she, as a child in the final months of World War II, suffered the bombing of her school by a strayed British airplane. The walls literally crashed down on her, killing a friend nearby and trapping her in rubble for many hours. How could she avoid nightmares of falling buildings?

I admire the Manhattan skyline from a distance. When walking through the concrete tunnels with the traffic and noise, wind, and pollution, I can't get a sense of the whole, can't see above ground level. But I do like the views from upper stories or a rooftop. A friend once had a pied-à-terre high in a building on Eighth Avenue in the fifties, with a perspective down past the tip of Battery Park to the Statue of Liberty. That was the right way to see the city.

The same friend took my wife and me to Windows on the World, the restaurant at the top of the World Trade Center, where we could dine and gaze over the harbor. He ate there often, called the servers by their first names, and got special attention.

I thought of that place and those people on 9-11, when all that elegance and all those lives came crashing down in gray clouds of debris. Perhaps the visiting woman knew the possibilities much better than we.

Still, I'm drawn to heights, though I was a bit apprehensive my first time up in a cable car suspended on a braided wire in the Swiss Alps. Watching the valley below, I contemplated the fall that would follow a snap, then took comfort in the reassurance that the entire contraption had been constructed by the same people who could make perfect watches. Once atop the peak of the Schilthorn Mountain, in the rotating Piz Gloria restaurant, I found myself rapt in looking out at the white crags of snow and ice that surrounded us. With great effort, humans had conquered some of the highest mountains in the world so that tourists like me could enjoy a hot meal and a view.

Yet it hadn't always been that way for travelers. The Alps had been a source of terror rather than awe. The fears of those people were justified in the days of horses and hiking, considering the frequency of avalanches, rock falls, blinding snowstorms, and bandits. Many travelers froze to death. Beyond the actual dangers, superstitions invented witches, dragons, and alien species lurking in the jagged massifs. Some of those who had no alternative to journeying across the peaks asked for blindfolds to shut out the threats, both real and imagined.

Now the Alps are a playground, paradise for skiers and hikers in the snow. I recall once climbing up many icy steps, thinking we were alone in the vastness, and discovering a roomful of happy pleasure seekers in an inn alive with food, drink, and gemütlichkeit.

Certainly, avalanches still happen, rocks come roaring down, earthquakes tumble buildings, planes drop bombs, fall out of the sky, stormy winds topple trees. Yet we can't wear literal or psychic blindfolds to shut out disaster. We can't shrink every building, ground every plane, level every mountain, and cut down every tree, especially trees as glorious as the one we had looked up to for so long. We should thrive among all that is above us.

Will Robots Displace Human Workers?

A ROBOT KILLED A YOUNG CONTRACTOR in a German Volkswagen production plant recently. While the worker was installing the stationary robot in its protective cage, the device suddenly struck out with a fatal blow. Apparently, this robot killing was the first of its kind in German manufacturing, with the greatest use of robots in Europe. In the United Kingdom, however, in 2007, 77 robot accidents were reported, with people crushed, hit on the head, welded, and doused with molten aluminum. Like the German robot, these were not the malevolent creations of sci-fi films but only machines misbehaving because of technical malfunctions. Was a crime committed at the Volkswagen plant? The local prosecutor's office is deciding "whether to bring charges, and, if so, against whom."

Should we humans be worried? I don't think so. At least, not about murderous production robots, whose responsibility for injuries and deaths equals only a fraction of the shower slips. For example, in 2007, 3,318 residents of the UK suffered fatal falls (not just when showering). That number dwarfs the 77 robot injuries, few—if any—of which were fatal.

But does that mean we should focus on shower mats and minding our steps rather than being concerned about robots and other products of artificial intelligence

(AI)? There, too, I don't think so.

While robots are not out to do us physical harm through acts of violent aggression, the consequences of AI algorithms are already affecting human life and are on the verge of even more consequential transformations. How deeply should this new reality concern us? The most extreme threat identified by a number of alarmed and famous scientists is human domination by a "race" of intelligent and self-replicating computerized devices, robotic and otherwise. A less existential possibility would have humans becoming superfluous for many occupations, and not just the production of Volkswagens and the like. On the list would be medicine, law, finance, and other fields that provide high salaries. What jobs would be left for creatures of flesh and blood?

Doomsday: The Singularity

Let's consider the worst-case scenario first. The physicist Stephen Hawking is quoted as warning:

> The development of full artificial intelligence could spell the end of the human race. It would take off on its own and re-design itself at an ever-increasing rate. Humans, who are limited by slow biological evolution, couldn't compete, and would be superseded.

Hawking's doomsday scenario is based on the AI concept of the "singularity"—the point at which the devices of artificial intelligence achieve the ability to surpass human mental processes; that is, to be smarter than we are. Ray Kurzweil, in *The Singularity Is Near*, predicts that non-biological intelligence will "soar" past that of humans. To prevent this possibility, Hawking has called for a cessation of extreme AI research and development.

If Hawking is right about the dangers, AI development—i.e. evolution—will move beyond the control of mankind and nature, possibly expanding at an exponential pace. Where it would all lead is beyond the imaginations of limited human brainpower, even the speculations of science-fiction masters who have dreamed up a host of dystopian futures.

AI Devices All Around Us

Yet, despite Hawking's plea, AI research and development is ongoing and progressing rapidly. We can see the results all around us, from voices on our smart phones that tell us how to get from one place to another or relieve us of the burden of dialing phone numbers—"Siri, call home"—to software that transmits automatic mortgage payments and manages our thermostats from miles away.

It's not only phone numbers we don't have to remember. Social media alerts us to family and friends' birthdays. Search engines offer facts and figures in mere seconds. Some consider these aids as paths to less rigorous minds, just as Plato's Socrates opposed writing because it obviated the need for memorization. He says in the *Phaedrus* that written text gives "the appearance of wisdom, not true wisdom." Similar criticisms have been made of the reliance on computers.

In the midst of writing this piece, I pause to search for references, verifications, and passages to quote. The resources of the Internet are at my fingertips, responding almost instantly. It's all too much for my limited brain. But one memory I do retain is driving to a library, flipping through a card catalogue, and running a finger over book spines to find the one that had the information I needed—a process of hours and days. Surely, computers have made life easier despite the pleasure of immersion in the stacks. Computers have become so ubiquitous—including the one I carry in a pocket—they may no longer seem examples of artificial intelligence. Note that the Word grammar tool has even restructured and improved several of my sentences, including one in this paragraph.

We live in a sea of devices that embody robotics and AI, as with computers, often taking them for granted. And many, if not most, of their devices are more effective and faster than humans at accomplishing tasks. Robots are better at manufacturing than people, and despite the poor victim at the VW plant, less dangerous to life and limb than human-operated machinery. Self-driven cars, now on the cusp of production, are also safer than person-driven cars. According to a McKinsey study reported in *Fast Company*, "autonomous vehicles could reduce traffic accidents by 90%. In the process, our new robot cars will save us $190 billion in wrecked cars, broken bones, and other costs incurred by plowing into things with our current fleet of brain-driven cars."

An immediate problem is the coexistence of robotic operators and human drivers who do not adhere to safety standards on the road. For example, Google cars have been in sixteen fender benders since 2009, all caused by humans at the wheel of the other vehicles, the company claims. A dark side exists: hacking into cars and controlling them, but that can happen even with a helpless human in the driver's seat, with a myriad of computerized processes, in fact.

Computerizing Occupational Functions

So, eventually people may interact with their cars just as they now rarely interact with a live person when calling a business organization. In fact, in the future people could even check into a hotel and have luggage delivered to their rooms without seeing another living soul. A Japanese hotel about to open uses an all-robot humanoid staff for check-in and machines to deliver baggage to rooms. Clearly, following the trend of manufacturing robots, automated answering, and driverless cars, robotics and AI can accomplish a range of tasks that once required human presence, especially including a very large number that provided gainful employment.

That's the possible variation of Stephen Hawking's doomsday scenario, not nearly as cataclysmic, but rather a chipping away at human work roles until many people will have fewer and fewer occupational functions.

Optimists and Pessimists

Such a pessimistic projection is hardly a given. Most of the pundits on the future of work for humans seem to share two extremes of an all-or-nothing mindset. For one group, robotics and AI will make the great majority of human workers obsolete and irrelevant. For the other group, the creations of the new technologies, most of which are not yet imagined, will yield an abundance of new careers, new opportunities, and new occupational satisfactions.

The Pew Research Center, in its 2014 *Future of the Internet Survey*, polled nearly 2,000 authorities about this question: "The economic impact of robotic advances and AI—Self-driving cars, intelligent digital agents that can act for you, and robots are advancing rapidly. Will networked, automated, artificial intelligence (AI) applications and robotic devices have displaced more jobs than they have created by 2025?" The responses split down the middle, with a slightly larger number—52 percent—on the optimistic side.

The pessimists saw widening income inequality, great numbers of unemployable, and social unrest. The optimists, while agreeing that robotic and AI technology will displace many workers, have "faith that human ingenuity will create new jobs, industries, and ways to make a living, just as it has been doing since the dawn of the Industrial Revolution." They argue that only humans can accomplish certain jobs.

Who Is at Risk?

But what are those jobs, and how long will they be immune to technological replacement? Will the as yet unknown new jobs provide employment for the millions displaced? Is the faith justified?

We already know about the predominance of robots in manufacturing and similar work based on their physical strength, dexterity, and singular focus. But what about mental occupations that require years of education and superior cognitive skills?

Let's take physicians, members of a profession with high prestige and high financial rewards, requiring many years of training and real intelligence to qualify. Yet they are vulnerable, too. At the M.D. Anderson Center, IBM's Watson supercomputer is being trained, i.e. programmed, to be a cancer specialist. If the experiment succeeds, Watson will take just minutes to process a patient's medical history, genetic data, tests, scans, and the like to determine an individualized plan of treatment. Medical researchers would require weeks to accomplish the same result.

Will AI replace doctors in other ways? Probably unlikely, but the doctor relationship with patients is already changing. The growing use of robotic surgeries—with the smaller incisions, less pain and bleeding, fewer infections, and faster healing times—has turned surgeons into control panel operators instead of hands-on scalpel wielders. Such procedures have been used for kidney and gallbladder removal, artery bypass, and cancer excision.

On an even smaller scale, NASA has developed a 0.4kg bot—microminiaturized robot—that can be inserted through the navel to perform abdominal surgery on astronauts in space if they suffer an unexpected malady like appendicitis or intestinal bleeding. The bots have a video camera and attachments to hold, cauterize, and suture tissue. An earthbound physician using joysticks would direct the procedure. So far, such surgeries have only been conducted on pigs. But, if they succeed, the use of bots would not have to be confined to those circling the earth.

Of course, robotic surgeries of any sort still need highly trained physicians to manage the controls. Is it possible that after the singularity—or even before—an AI algorithm could take over?

Psychiatrists, with their hourly rates, may be more vulnerable in some areas. An experimental computer program can diagnose depression, a condition often unrecognized. The method analyzes speech patterns and uses tracking cameras to measure facial expressions and eye movements during conversation. The algorithm has been 75 percent effective in the resulting diagnoses. Of course, a human would be necessary to follow up with therapy and medications. So far.

An even more impressive computerized psychiatric diagnostic result is found in the 100% accuracy of an automated speech-analysis program that differentiated between young at-risk people who became psychotic and those who did not over a two-and-a-half year period. The computer's predictive accuracy was far greater than methods such as neuroimaging and EEG measurement of brain activity.

Lawyers aren't exempt from AI replacement. A report in *The New York Times* uses the example of a 1978 Justice Department lawsuit where "discovery" involved examining 6 million documents by lawyers and paralegals at a cost of $2.2 million. In contrast, recently, "e-discovery" software analyzed 1.5 million documents for less than $100.000. Like Watson for cancer, this software did the job in a fraction of the time. Less than 60% of 2014 graduates had found jobs in the field after ten months of search. Yet law schools keep turning them out, perhaps to maintain a flow of tuition income, ignoring the consequences of AI.

Even the highly lucrative world of financial services

is on the cusp of widespread computerization, according to an article in the *Harvard Business Review* by Brad Power, a consultant at FCB Partners. He reports that Watson Group Marketing Communications has clients working mostly on three applications: a virtual agent that banks and insurance companies can use for "personalized" customer relationship, a wealth planning advisor, and a tool for risk and compliance management. USAA, another financial services organization, uses the Enhanced Virtual Assistant, or Eva, which, according to Neff Hudson, vice president of emerging channels, "enables members to do 200 transactions by just talking, including transferring money and paying bills. It makes search easier and answers in a Siri-like voice. But this is a 1.0 version. Our next step is to create a virtual agent that is capable of learning."

What's happening at the Watson Group seems to be an illustration of one of the conclusions reached by Paul Rowady of the Tabb Group: that the financial market will shift expenditures from people to technology and replace financial specialists with those who develop and manage this technology. According to Rowady, "We see the true and blunt objective of digital transformation as the elimination of dependence on human responsibility for tasks and processes wherever possible." The result will be an industry-wide reduction in head count and shifts to new skillsets for the employees who remain.

Replaced workers in fields such as medicine, law, and finance will be just one aspect of the transformation ahead, according to Richard and Daniel Suskind in their soon-to-be-published book, *The Future of the Professions: How Technology Will Transform the Work of*

Human Experts. They predict a decline of today's professions in an Internet society: "… we will neither need nor want doctors, teachers, accountants, architects, the clergy, consultants, lawyers, and many others, to work as they did in the 20th century." Technology will bring an upheaval to what professionals do and how they do it.

Winners and Losers

In its report on the future of work at a time of AI and automation, *The Economist* includes a table that lists certain occupations and the likelihood of their replacement as a result of computerization. The source was C. Frey and M. Osborne's 2013 calculations, "The Future of Employment: How Susceptible are Jobs to Computerisation." Their news is bad for telemarketers, accountants and auditors, retail salespersons, technical writers, real estate agents, among others. It's middling for machinists, commercial pilots, health technologists, and economists. Editors and chemical engineers seem safe. But safest of all, and likely to increase, are recreational therapists, dentists, athletic trainers, and clergy. The latter suggests a growing need for prayer in the future.

The Economist concludes: "However, society may find itself sorely tested if, as seems possible, growth and innovation deliver handsome gains to the skilled, while the rest cling to dwindling employment opportunities at stagnant wages." Such dislocation is not a hypothesis in light of the evidence from recent economic growth. The profits soar to those already at the top. Most people belong to "the rest."

The Fate of Workers in a Robotic Age

What will happen to the unemployed and the growing numbers of underemployed if that assessment, along with those of the Pew pessimists, plays out in the future?

According to one scenario, "the rest" have nothing to worry about if AI devices come to dominate productive functions. A rosy view sees an accumulating abundance of wealth resulting from the economic productivity of a robotic workforce. These riches would allow governments to support "the rest" through grants and the comforting supports of social services. Assuming that food, sustenance, and shelter vanish as human concerns, then what?

Two radically different alternative consequences of such prosperity have been suggested. In one, content people will indulge in the fruits of their leisure, happy to become clients of all those new recreational therapists. They'll travel, swim, read, listen to music, and cultivate all their real and psychological gardens.

The unhappy opposite has them wallowing in functionless boredom, aimless and depressed, not unlike retired people who no longer have work to occupy their time and to sustain their psyches. Sue Halpern, in her *New York Review of Books* review of Nicholas Carr's *The Glass Cage: Automation and Us*, cites a finding by Dean Baker of the Center for Economic and Policy Research that the death rate for older males goes up significantly soon after they stop working. Carr cites a conclusion made in 1990 by Mihaly Csikszentmihalyi, the author of *Flow: The Psychology of Optimal Experience*, that "people were happier, felt more fulfilled by what they were doing, while they were at work than during their leisure hours."

Marcus Wohlsen, a senior writer at *Wired*, wonders what would happen if people didn't have to work:

> The idea that robots could make employment itself optional may sound fantastic. No more work! But the end result could be more, not less angst. We'd still have to find our place among the robots, except this time without work as a guidepost for defining a sense of purpose. By eliminating the need for people to work, robots would free us up to focus on what really makes us human. The scariest possibility of all is that only then do we figure out what really makes us human is work.

Existential anxiety may be the least of it for great numbers of unemployed, particularly millions of young people at the peak of hormonal urgings.

The extent of actual unemployment today, especially of the young, has been posited as a reason for radical violence in the Middle East, with religion just an excuse. Interviews of a number of people who have gravitated to ISIL reveal that the cause gives them a function and a purpose—conquest rather than aimlessness.

According to John Brian Shannon, an editor at *Arabian Gazette of Dubai*, "Unemployment among youths continues to hit 70% in some Middle East countries. It's not a temporary situation; it's the normal state of affairs there, and almost alone it's responsible for the rapid rise of terror and other crime throughout the region."

A far less warlike possibility is dramatized in Kurt Vonnegut's 1952 dystopian novel, *Player Piano*, in which the protagonist, Paul Proteus, claims, "Machines and organization and pursuit of efficiency have robbed the American people of liberty and the pursuit of happiness." At the climax, bands of angry unemployed destroy the machines that replaced them, but ultimately—with nothing else to do—turn to rebuilding them to give themselves a purpose.

I'm also reminded of Dostoevsky (a writer whose work influenced Vonnegut's) and his Underground Man, who—despite his many maladjustments—is often admirably perceptive. Two of his insights are relevant to the question of whether people need work. He asserts that they will commit to meaningless tasks just to be saved from "the deadly snares of idleness." And "The whole work of man really seems to consist in nothing but proving to himself every minute that he is a man and not a piano key." Vonnegut's unemployed reject roles as the pedal pumpers of player pianos that create the real music. Yet, in the end all they have is make-work.

Another author who comes to mind is Henry David Thoreau, who wrote in his *Journal* of "the most poetical farmer": "He does nothing with haste and drudgery, but as if he loved it. He makes the most of his labor, and takes infinite satisfaction in every part of it. He is not looking forward to the sale of his crops or any pecuniary profit, but he is paid by the constant satisfaction which his labor yields him." Perhaps Thoreau would agree that there is only "quiet desperation" in being a piano key.

Sources

"Monty": *World Heritage Encyclopedia article on Anybots,* via Project Gutenberg. Honda: *7 Jobs That Can Be Done By A*

Robot, by David Schepp, Aol Jobs, 2011 [with infographic from Mindflash.com]. Danger: *Beyond R2-D2: Australian manufacturing's robotics wish-list*, by Peter Kambouris, The Conversation, 2013. Trumpeters: *Xconomy Forum: Robots Remake the Workplace on April 11*, by Renee Blodgett, We Blog the World, 2013.

Fyodor Dostoevsky, *Notes from Underground*. Translated by Constance Garnett. Barnes and Noble Classics, 2008.

Rory Cellan-Jones. "Stephen Hawking warns artificial intelligence could end mankind." BBC, December 2, 2014 Accessed via bbc.com/news.

Aaron Smith and Janna Anderson. "AI, Robotics, and the Future of Jobs." Pew Research Center. pewinternet.org/2014/08/06/future-of-jobs.

Ariana Eunjung Cha. "Watson's next feat? Taking on cancer." *Washington Post*, June 27, 2015. *The Economist*. "The future of jobs." January 18, 2014. Donald M. Fiene. "Elements of Dostoevsky in the Novels of Kurt Vonnegut." Sue Halpern. "How Robots & Algorithms Are Taking Over." *New York Review of Books*, April 2, 2015.

Steven J. Harperaug. "Too Many Law Students, Too Few Legal Jobs." *New York Times*, August 25, 2015.

Ray Kurzweil. *The Singularity Is Near*. Viking Press, 2006.

Adrienne LaFrance. "Computers Can Predict Schizophrenia Based on How a Person Talks." *The Atlantic*. August 26, 2015.

John Markoff. "Armies of Expensive Lawyers, Replaced by Cheaper Software." *The New York Times*, March 4, 2011.

Rick Noack. "A robot killed a factory worker in Germany. So who should go on trial?" *The Washington Post*, July 2, 2015.

Maria Popova. "Thoreau on Hard Work, the Myth of Productivity, and the True Measure of Meaningful Labor." *Brain Pickings*.

Brad Power. "Artificial Intelligence Is Almost Ready for Business." *Harvard Business Review*, March 19, 2015.

"Robotic Surgery." *Medline Plus*.

Richard and Daniel Suskind. *The Future of the Professions: How Technology Will Transform the Work of Human Experts*.

Oxford University Press, 2015.

John Paul Titlow. "Self-Driving Cars Will Be the Biggest Auto Safety Innovation Ever." *Fast Company*, March 5, 2015.

Matt Turner, "The robot revolution is coming for Wall Street traders." *Business Insider*, August 17, 2015.

James Vincent. "Surgery in space: Nasa helps develop Matrix-like robot that slips in through your belly button." *The Independent*, April 3, 2014.

Kurt Vonnegut. *Player Piano*. The Dial Press, 1999.

Marcus Wohlsen. "When Robots Take All The Work, What'll Be Left For Us To Do?" *Wired*, August 8, 2014.

Economic Responsibility: Covid and Social Darwinism

Who bears the responsibility if a person who works a full-time job cannot afford rent, food, and medical care? Or even worse, if a person cannot even find a job. Typically, society—especially American society—blames the individual for being at fault, and in many cases, individuals blame themselves, as is evident from the despair of opioid addition and suicides among unemployed working-class men, people punishing themselves for the failure to provide for themselves and their families.

The Covid-19 pandemic, however, has undermined the assumptions that place the blame on the individual. Millions of jobs disappeared within a matter of months through no fault of the people who lost them because mandates to avoid crowds led to the shutting down of restaurants, retail outlets, small stores, gyms, offices, and schools. The many subsisting from paycheck to paycheck found themselves unable to survive, having a place to live only because of eviction bans, spending hours in long lines for donated foods.

These millions knew their plight hadn't resulted from anything they did. They were economic victims of a virus. But Covid unleashed a consideration of the larger ongoing questions about economic responsibility. What are the real causes of unemployment and under-employment? Are deficient individuals the reason, or are their circumstances the result of forces over which they have no control? If not by a disease, is their economic status determined by the nature of the economy and decisions of those with the power to set the rules for that economy?

For many years, the attitudes of the larger American society have been based on vestiges of Social Darwinism, which assumes that economic failure is a sign of some inferiority or inadequacy. And Social Darwinism relates to the Calvinist premises of the elect, those chosen by God for salvation and eternal life. The Victorian mill owners who exploited workers, even small children, for long, brutal hours six days a week, used a conflation of those theories to justify this abuse for profit. God had chosen them to be the wealthy owners and had condemned the workers to penury by some form of divine prejudgment.

Even if the term Social Darwinism may not be current today, its premises have dominated American attitudes toward the unemployed and the poor, especially those on welfare. They are considered unworthy, much lesser beings than those existing in affluent comforts. But the premises of Social Darwinism are based on a perversion of Darwinian evolutionary theory.

Darwin himself posited that creatures most adaptable to existing circumstances were those who survived and whose traits passed onto future generations. One of his best-known examples involves birds in a time of drought, when the worms are deeper in the ground in search of moisture. Birds with longer beaks were able to penetrate farther into the earth in search of food. They survived while birds with short beaks starved. The long beak offspring became the future of the species, demonstrating the nature of evolutionary theory. They were not better birds, just fortunate to possess the right traits for the time. If effect, they survived because of happenstance and luck. Darwin used the term "natural selection."

The process because transposed into "survival of the fittest" by Herbert Spencer in his 1864 book *Principles of Biology*: "This survival of the fittest, which I have here sought to express in mechanical terms, is that which Mr. Darwin has called 'natural selection', or the preservation of favoured races in the struggle for life." Darwin himself accepted the phrase in future writings.

But Spencer also had an economic and political agenda behind his wording; for example, "Thus by survival of the fittest, the militant type of society becomes characterized by profound confidence in the governing power, joined with a loyalty causing submission to it in all matters whatever."

The implication of Spencer's concept, which was not what Darwin meant, when applied to human beings argues that some races are better than others and some people fitter than others, a moral judgment of superiority in line with the notion of Calvinist elect rather than the accidental good fortune of a long beak.

Spencer was writing during the time of the growth of Victorian mills when the owners exerted great power over workers because of high unemployment and lack of worker bargaining power. Most people—including women and children—worked between 12 and 16 hours per day, six days a week in abysmal conditions for low wages. The mill owners, whose goal was amassing more personal wealth, rationalized this exploitation though a version of Social Darwinism. Workers suffered miserable lives because they were inferior beings deserving of their lot, while the owners had been chosen to enjoy lives of luxury in mansions.

While in most of the advanced world today workers are far less exploited than those in the Victorian mills, with shorter workdays, some benefits, and more sanitary conditions, the equivalents to long and short beaks still determine social and economic status.

I'll use myself as an example of how the timing of attributes and circumstances could have been the basis of my economic status.

After my graduation from high school, I found a summer job in the warehouse of the local tile factory, arranging boxes with the various types and colors of tiles on the appropriate racks. It meant stooping, lifting, and carrying. I am not very big or very strong. Halfway through the summer I threw my back out, with lifelong consequences, and could no longer do the work. Let's say I had been living at a time in history when my only employment opportunities were some version of hauling boxes, I'd have been in the same dire condition as a bird with a short beak.

Fortunately, the tile factory was not my future. I was heading off to college that fall where, after some groping, my educational beak caught the equivalent of a worm. I was lucky enough to survive. That was when a minority of Americans attended college.

Now college has become a necessity because of the

economic rewards dependent on a degree, the great gaps in lifetime income totals for those with degrees compared with those with high school graduates and, even worse, those who did not complete high school. In effect, the degree makes one fitter and a grad school degree even more so. Yet many are not college material or can't afford the costs if they are.

The question behind these income calculations is one of fairness. Do those with the ability to complete college and grad school deserve that much more than the dropouts consigned to some form of hauling boxes? Who determines the economic value of being a, say, senior vice president and, say, a warehouse worker?

Society likes to pretend there's some fair objective system of income distribution in making such an evaluation. But the reality is similar to that of the Victorian mill. Those with the power to set pay rates calculate how little they can get away with paying those with limited options so that those on the top can accumulate more profits for their own rewards. We see this result even more so in recent years as those at the top accumulate more and more wealth while the middle class shrinks and those at the bottom stagnate. Those who benefit most justify their fortunes as a form of economic natural selection.

They also tend to believe that people like them—people who live in similar neighborhoods with similar lifestyles—deserve more than people unlike them. For example, my late wife worked for a pharmaceutical company where most of those in higher management rose from careers in marketing. They had the higher salaries, the fancier offices, the pampering perks, while the scientists actually developing drugs—designated "lab rats"—often worked in basement facilities and had to switch to careers in management if they wanted to earn more and increase their future economic prospects.

The managers were also the people who received annual bonuses and took long lunches, unlike the clerical staff with limited opportunities to leave their desks and none to earn extra rewards. The assumption for this difference is a judgment that upper management is fitter.

In truth, what people are paid bears minimal relationship to the value of what they do on their job. In part, it's determined by what it costs to get people to take certain jobs. But in the main, it's paying as little as those in charge can get away with, the less the better for bottom line profits.

Occasionally, that less is the most certain businesses, mainly small ones, can afford and still survive. Restaurants are one of the small businesses in that category. Many fail and many others just squeak by. Covid-19 shutdowns closed thousands and eliminated millions of jobs, even though those jobs are low-paying.

I hear much about the frustrations of running a restaurant from a daughter who has been in that business for several decades, for most of them working seven days a week for ten or twelve hours a day, constantly hassled by employees who don't show or waste time bickering.

Because the pay is low, one would think restaurant work is a refuge for the unskilled, those willing to take minimum wage. It's not that simple. Work in a hot kitchen can be hectic, requiring energy and the ability to multitask. Jobs that involve serving, answering phones, and standing at the cash register involve my daughter in weeks—sometimes months—of training. Yet she frequently finds people who are not trainable and has to let them go after a trial period.

Their inability raises the question of what to do with people like me in my tile warehouse career, people who lack the qualifications for even menial tasks. And the number of menial task jobs are shrinking as robotics and machines do the heavy lifting and digging, while many of the jobs that are left require some level of computer skills. Consider how the military, which at one time was a refuge for the unskilled, by now has admission requirements because even using a weapon calls for training and knowledge.

What do we do about the people who lack the dexterity or aptitude for the low-level jobs that remain? Do we consign them to a future of extinction like short-billed birds that cannot feed themselves? And what of people who work full-time, but because of the cost of housing and other expenses where they live, do not earn enough to pay for rent, fuel, groceries, and doctor visits? In most areas of the U.S., despite minimum wage mandates, large numbers of people fail to earn enough to meet their expenses. Minimum wage is not a living wage.

From the perspective of Social Darwinism, such people bear the responsibility for their economic inadequacies because they are ultimately unfit. But let's assume the compensation these people receive for their work or even their inability to find work is ultimately determined by forces over which they have no control. In such an economic reality, the inaccessibility of the worm beyond their reach is not their fault. If the system is the real reason for their struggles, does society bear a responsibility to make sure they have food, shelter, and medical care?

Before Covid-19, the consensus probably was no. Society should intervene in only the worse cases of deprivation. After Covid-19, when so many who had demonstrated their fitness over time ended up losing jobs and businesses, a new consensus can agree that individuals often do not have control of their destinies.

The Economist magazine, long a champion of the free market, now accepts that "The pandemic has forced a re-evaluation of the social contract, in particular how risk should be divided among individuals, employers and the state." It calls for new thinking about social safety nets and the attitudes behind them, noting that the spending to prop up individuals has become a necessity rather than a begrudged handout. Governments have a role in underwriting risks. *The Economist* concludes, "The impact of climate change, technological innovations and demographic shifts on jobs and livelihoods is hard to predict. But further social disruption is almost certain. Better preparations cannot start soon enough."

Returning to the Darwinian example, the short-beaked birds should not be blamed for their inability to reach the worm. Instead, society should provide them with a tool to dig down further to reach the sustenance essential for survival or simply admit that the system is rigged and distribute worms to the hungry.

Meaningless Work

BECAUSE MY CAREER HAS BEEN as a university teacher, I've had only a tangential relationship to the world of what most people would call work. Yet my own experiences and reports from others who have spent a lifetime in that world convince me of massive waste—days, weeks, and years consumed in roles that are essentially make-believe, resulting in paychecks but accomplishing little of real value to society.

Immediately after college I spent a few years in the corporate realm and, during my teaching years, moonlighted as a consultant. Then there were the many hours my late wife and I devoted to discussing her frustrated reports of her own consulting experiences with several major corporations. She accumulated example after example of people playing roles and killing time.

The late British anthropologist David Graeber of the London School of Economics called these occupations "bullshit jobs" in a 2013 article for the UK magazine *Strike*, asserting, "Huge swathes of people, in Europe and North America in particular, spend their entire working lives performing tasks they secretly believe do not really need to be performed." He cites a whole class of salaried professionals who will at parties "launch into tirades about how pointless and stupid their job really is."

Strike identifies itself as a publication that seeks to change the existing social order under capitalism. But Graeber expanded his article into the book *Bullshit Jobs* published by Simon and Shuster in 2018. The physicist Mark Buchanan, in *Bloomberg Magazine* that year, endorses and echoes Graeber in his article "Too Many Jobs Feel Meaningless Because They Are." He comments on Graeber's assertion that 30% of jobs contribute nothing to society:

> It might seem an obnoxious claim, if not for the fact that a huge number of people willingly attest to the worthlessness of their own jobs. A 2015 U.K. survey found that 37% of people felt their jobs "did not make a meaningful contribution to the world," and a later poll in the Netherlands found 40% saying the same thing.

From my own anecdotal experiences and indirect knowledge, that may be an undercount. What's key here is what one defines as a contribution to society. What does humanity really need? What eases our lives? What diverts and amuses? What involves empty hours? And what does damage?

The ability to consider one's job meaningless may be elitist, a luxury of the middle class and affluent. Their work doesn't call for immediate outcomes and usually involves planning for the future. These positions seem to call for more education and knowledge, resulting in higher pay. The less-educated and low-paid who serve food, mow lawns, deliver packages, clean homes, etc. perform work that has a direct consequence. Does that imply a form of meaning? Which jobs inherently matter, and which are extraneous?

No question that we need food, shelter, garments, and healthcare. But do we need artery clogging BigMacs or the wasted space of MacMansions? Do we need tobacco farms and cigarettes? Legal marijuana growing? Gasoline engines that help us get to shopping malls but cause destructive climate change? For that matter, does society really need the subjects I've spent decades teaching?

What about teaching, something I did for decades? We have administrative bosses who approve our contract renewals and promotions. But our interactions with them are occasional, often many months apart. Our more pertinent contacts are the frequent sessions with students, some of whom find our classes meaningful, others who yawn through them or just cut. We strive to make our courses matter to everyone in the room, disappointed when they don't, fulfilled when they do.

But for even the most dedicated student, classes are only part of their college experience, mixed with bull sessions, parties, playing a sport, searching for short- or long-term partners, and—eventually—being handed a diploma that would lead to a job, preferably one that isn't just well-paying make-work.

Another way of asking the question about job usefulness can avoid the measure of defining a real contribution by asking whether the work brings satisfaction to the person doing it. At the heart of the matter is the sense of accomplishment. For example, organizing my desk contributes nothing to the world but makes me feel that I've done something useful.

I imagine a similar inner glow for the engineers, technicians, and programmers who created the M1 chip for the MacBook laptop with a great increase in speed and battery life, even though in the larger scheme of things it's a minor blip. Perhaps the research kitchen staff that succeeded in squeezing more calories into a BigMac share a similar inner glow. They strove and met a goal.

But what if these goal-meeters, in the bright light of day or dark night of the soul, are shaken by the realization that a few hours of battery life or another strip of bacon are ultimately meaningless. Will they join those—the perhaps 37 to 40%—who are aware as they travel to their jobs that the day ahead will be futile.

The social and occupational upheaval resulting from the Covid-19 pandemic has led millions to acknowledge their work frustrations. Unable to enter their workplaces or confined to specific hours at desks and workstations, they have had time to think, leading a significant proportion to quit what they were doing and seek more fulfilling alternatives.

"People with meaningful work flourish. People without it suffer," concludes Joe Keohane in "What is Meaningful Work" from the January/February 2022 issue of *Entrepreneur.* His interviews with academic and business professionals underline the benefits for employees and organizations but the difficulties in coming up with a definition that identifies the characteristics that explain jobs with meaning. Most likely, it's a matter of individual perception. People want to feel that they are being useful and that what they do matters.

But that could be a delusion, a self-deception to make the day tolerable. The realization resulting from the time to think during the isolation of Covid has been the reason millions have joined the Great Resignation from existing jobs and changed the definition of "matters" for so many.

I, who have never held a regular job beyond lifting tite boxes, busing tables at summer resorts, or sitting at a bookstore cash register, came to that conclusion a few months after college graduation when in my first position at a major corporati0n. I was on a track to upper management and soon knew I didn't want to get there.

My initial assignment was proofreading instruction manuals for the ships' turbines manufactured in a building deep in the rabbit warren of structures packed into General Electric's Schenectady works. Anonymous engineers wrote the manuals and subcontracted typists with IBM Selectrics turned out the two-column pages I had to check for typos and reference codes that fulfilled precise specifications. A glum, unsmiling man would appear regularly to check our proofing as if meeting those specifications were matters of life and death significance. My fellow trainees and I feared his nitpicking.

Those two columns had to be right margin justified, something that can be done instantaneously with computer word processing today. Back then the Selectric came up with the number of hairline spaces that had to be inserted into each line to produce justification. The first version we proofed had to be retyped with those insertions, and we had to proofread all over again. I assume those anonymous typists—perhaps working at home in a version of cottage industry—were happy to be paid for their keyboarding. I was being paid for my contributions to the process. But even then, even in my raw youth, I wondered why we were all bothering to devote so many hours to the look of justification that had no connection to content.

My workstation was a desk in a cubicle shared with three other trainees who agreed about the tediousness of our assignment. Out of boredom, we spent half the workday looking down at our desktops but having conversations about sports and movies or playing hang-the-man on empty sheets of company paper. When, after several months, it came to having our productivity evaluated, I feared the consequences of our shirking. But no fear. It turned out that the four of us had the best productivity rate of years of predecessors who occupied those same desks. We wondered how they could have wasted more time than we did.

Occasionally, I had the opportunity to step inside the office of someone with a management title, a person who had made it past the trainee stage and one or two internal promotions. Depending on their titles, they had better wooden desks instead of our metal, carpeted floors, and bigger windows. The papers on their desktops were neatly stacked. I wondered what they did all day and eventually learned they spent their time assigning tasks to people below them and making sure everyone stayed within their budget projections. They did no real work themselves.

That, I realized, was the future laying ahead for me—plusher offices and bigger budgets to fret over. I'd also have the growing salary for a better and better car and bigger and bigger house. Such a future scared me. I decided had to find a new life as soon as I could invent an escape. That's when it occurred to me to apply to graduate school, a possibility I had never once considered while an undergraduate.

But the immediate future weeks ahead was six months active duty in the National Guard. I had to linger at GE until my reporting date came up. Coincidentally, I was released from ships' turbines and given the task of coordinating proposals for multi-million-dollar projects for the company's Missile and Space Vehicle division.

That meant one-hundred-hour weeks at the division's headquarters in Philadelphia, begging engineers to release their sections in time to meet a rigid deadline. To complicate matters, the work was classified and had to be tracked, signed off, and locked away every night. But this was the challenge of real work, me managing multiple urgencies, fueled by caffeine and adrenalin.

Printed copies of my first proposal made the deadline by the whisker of a few hours, my reward a day off and a whisper that I had a future with the company. But, more significantly, I told myself I had accomplished something real, far more vital than right margin justification. That is, until one day in the lunchroom when I, by chance, sat with a manager I knew only casually.

"You," he said once we exchanged greetings, "coordinated the Subroc proposal."

I nodded, restraining an instinct to unload the hundreds of anxious hours.

He shrugged. "We were never going to get that contract. It was Raytheon's turn. That's the way the government works. They alternate the winners. But we have to make a show and turn in a proposal."

My lunch tasted like the paper plate. My stressed hours had been a hollow pretense. I knew I'd never want a future with that company or any company. The National Guard provided an immediate escape.

During the six months of basic training, I polished brass, shined boots, and shoved a cleaning rod down the barrel of an M1 rifle, aware that none of it mattered. Back in civvies I notified GE I wouldn't be back and took an editing job at a tech writing firm in New York while applying to grad schools.

At that firm my supervisor, a plump, cologned man, had no idea what he was doing or what I should be doing. He advised me to take initiative, which meant spending my purposeless workday cleaning out filing cabinets. Eventually, that led me to discover hundreds of billing hours had been charged to the creation of manuals for GE's radar division in Syracuse. With not one manual started and a deadline two weeks away, I expected my supervisor to panic.

Instead, he told me I would fly to Syracuse and concoct a reason why we were so far behind; that is, play the role of someone who had the slightest idea about radar systems. In absolute confusion, I made the flight with no idea what I would say. My host there, a pleasant, pipe-smoking engineer, didn't give me a chance to stammer any lame excuse, taking me into a domed building and showing off the radar system with obvious pride, while I nodded as if I knew what he was talking about.

Then, as I was about to apologize for our delay, he stopped me and made his own apology. "We should have notified you months ago about all the changes we've made. Specs are all different now. Your manual drafts are obsolete. You're going to have to start almost from scratch. I really apologize." Puff, puff.

Not only did I get away with pretending to be a radar engineer, but my firm was also going to get much more money and months of extension. An empty triumph. It turned out that the radar manuals were not the firm's only screwup. It folded a few weeks after my roleplay. We got no severance.

My wife's consulting career found her performing parallel roleplaying, though not deceiving the people she worked for, instead actually doing what they wanted. That was when she was a speech writer for company executives, presidents and vice presidents. Initially, when assigned a topic for an important audience, she scheduled an interview with the executive, only to be told, "I don't know much about subject. Come up with something."

What she came up with often became institutionalized as company policy, mainly because she had common sense and figured out what seemed logical. Proof of this came when she was hired to write speeches for the woman who had been named president of a newly created Johnson & Johnson company. The woman handed my wife a copy of a speech given by the president of another company, emphatically and repeatedly insisting that she wanted it as a model for her own speeches. "Have you read it?" she asked my wife as if she should be ashamed if she hadn't. With a straight face, my wife told her "I wrote it."

My wife really was interested in pharmaceutical research. One day, when she gave her supervisor an enthusiastic report on a new finding of potential significance, the woman gave her a blank look and said, "Do I have to know this?"

During my own moonlighting sessions held when I had breaks from teaching, one of my assignments was a full week on writing improvement for Western Electric, a now-defunct division of the old iteration of AT&T. Coincidentally, my wife consulted for AT&T and was well aware that departments in the company spent almost all their time at war with other departments, paying almost no attention to external changes in the telecommunication industry that would soon undermine their business model.

At one of my Western Electric weeks a young woman in the group complained, "I spent a whole year working on a project that was suddenly cancelled. Everything I did for those months was wasted."

The middle-aged men in the class burst out laughing until one finally said, "I've been with the company twenty years, and no project I've worked on has ever been finished." The others all nodded and grinned. In short, they had spent their professional lives killing time and getting paid for it.

In a world of bullshit jobs, millions of employees are probably happy to fill the day for a regular salary. They don't care if they were doing anything useful. Their lives are fulfilled by being able to afford devotion to avocations like gardening, fishing, bowling, cooking, watching football—free-time compensations for tedious job-time duties.

But there may be another reason some tolerate what their job obligations. These people may regard their work as a game with absolutely no connection to a real purpose. The assignment is considered self-contained, some sort of puzzle to be solved just for the sake of solving. For example, if I had been content of with a career of turning our useless proposals for contracts that were already predetermined, my satisfaction would have been passing the test of gathering all the content and meeting the deadlines. Like assembling a thousand-piece puzzle or winning at hang-the-man.

In fact, I took that perspective to some moonlighting projects that lacked any connection with my real profession. For example, my managerial contact at a supermarket's headquarters asked me to produce an operating manual for checkout cashiers. It meant extra money for me and wouldn't take all that long. Still, I wanted to do good work because I liked the woman who was my contact. Any failure on my part would reflect on her. Hundreds of copies of the manual I turned out were printed. Months later, when I asked my contact what workers thought of them, she gave a knowing wince and told me they were still stacked her boss's closet. Not long after, that supermarket chain went out of business. My work may be still closeted under thick dust in an empty building.

My experiences, unique as they may be, leave open the question of how many of us are really engaged in significant employment. What jobs are not bullshit? What buildings deserve to be empty?

Downton Abbey and the End of a Way of Life

DOWNTON ABBEY HAS BEEN A TV PHENOMENON, with audiences in more than 200 countries, including 160 million viewers in China. In the U.S. it is the most popular PBS program ever, and, during the 2014-15 viewing year, it came out twentieth in popularity among all network and cable programming, just behind *Monday Night Football.*

Why has it had such broad appeal? It's difficult—perhaps impossible—to generalize for the planet, for viewers in places as disparate as Saskatoon and Shanghai. At the root, the series does dramatize a range of human stories—love, birth, death, mendacity, betrayal, grief, hope. But so do many films and TV programs. Why *Downton Abbey* and not a show that isn't a costume drama? More specifically, why does it have such appeal for nearly ten million Americans?

Millions of Americans are falling out of the middle class. Against this grim reality, the appeal of *Downton Abbey* and its final season.

Various commentators have speculated. *TV Guide* in January 2013 offered six reasons, among them that the upper-class soap opera plot makes us feel classy, that we're captivated by love stories with uncertain outcomes, and that we indulge in "materialistic voyeurism."

"We're in a similar situation economically and social-ly," the *Guide* proposes, noting that *Downton* episodes have focused on women's rights, sexual liberation, class aspirations, health care, and questions of egalitarianism. American viewers can relate to struggles that explore many changes of our own recent decades and, in some cases, matters that remain unresolved.

Yet the list above overlooks what may be a more visceral viewer connection: the fundamental social and economic upheavals now underlying Americans' deepest anxieties. In 2015-16, millions of Americans are falling out of the middle class. The same manu-facturing jobs that, one hundred years ago, sustained Britain's former servants have disappeared. Higher education no longer guarantees prosperity, and some experts argue that the U.S. will never again experi-ence the soaring economic growth of the twentieth century. Inequality grows as the profits that corpo-rations continue to realize now go primarily to the 1%. Against this grim reality, the appeal of *Downton Abbey* may be based in the darker undercurrent of economic decline which lurks beneath the character's stories and blurs into ours.

Ultimately, despite the nostalgic surface, *Down-ton Abbey* is about the end of a way of life. The seeds of decline were planted in the very first season with the uncertainty of who would be heir to the estate. And there was the backstory: like many other British aristo-cratic families of the time, the family needed to be res-cued financially by Lord Grantham marrying a wealthy American. In this final season, the squeeze on Downton finances receives more attention, primarily through frequent reminders of the shrinking servant staff.

That's no surprise. It's a matter of history. We know what happened to those great estates and all the servants who pampered the owners and kept the establishments running. To an extent never duplicated in the U.S., positions as servants at Britain's estates once were a major source of jobs. At the beginning of the twentieth century, domestic work was the country's largest employment category, with one and one half million people engaged as maids, cooks, waiters, valets, butlers, laundresses, gardeners, gatekeepers, stable-lads, chauffeurs, etc. By the middle of the twentieth century, however, the vast majority had migrated to fill other jobs—jobs that offered equivalent compensation for shorter workdays and the opportunity to live private lives in their own homes with their own families. Perhaps most importantly, they appreciated the opportunity to fulfill individual aspirations thanks to the range of employment possibilities.

By 2015 the number of domestic workers in the U.K .numbered only 65,000, the great majority in the category of independent contractors working for multiple employers, rarely living in some vestige of servants' quarters.

Aristocratic estate owners also became anachronisms. For centuries they had financed their extravagant lifestyles from the profits of the crops grown on their vast land holdings, and they were aided by the high tariffs that were imposed on imported crops. But those tariffs ended with a reform act in the late 1800s. Britain's scales tipped in favor of manufacturing and commercial enter-

prises, with a new group of rich—often from humble origins—taking charge. By the 1920s, aristocratic families
felt the heavy burdens of death duties and high taxes.

Few estates could afford to exist without their doors
being opened to paying visitors or the property being
rented out for events and to be used as film and TV
sets. A few were even turned into theme parks with jungle animals. More than a thousand grand homes were
demolished. Some aristocrats, keeping their titles but
not their former power and prestige, still live in corners
of their ancestors' great houses and devote their days to
maintaining an income stream, obsolescent remainders
of what was.

The series is diverting to watch. The furnishings are
elegant, the multiple plots are seductive, and the characters enjoy happy endings by the final show, almost every
one pairing off in love and marriage, and with babies on
their way. It's yet another replication of Shakespearean
comedy in which a world temporarily gone awry finds its
way to a satisfying equilibrium, purged of the unsettling
elements and promising a contented future.

Yet, knowing history—and thus knowing what will
happen to these people and their estate—we watch the
series's fictionally satisfying conclusion with an edge of dramatic irony. The apparent survival of the Downton Abbey
world, constrained as it may be, is an illusion. In the 1920s
that world was already coming undone, notwithstanding
the happy festivities that conclude the TV series. It would be
gone by the middle of the twentieth century.

In 2016, a way of life that tens of millions of Americans once enjoyed also appears to be collapsing. But

unlike the residents of the Abbey—particularly the servants—who went on to other, often satisfying, occupations, finding new careers and comforts, we have no idea where we will end up. Our futures lack the hopes our predecessors enjoyed. And a TV series is only a brief diversion.

Sources

Sadie Gennis, "Six Reasons Why Americans Are So Bloody Obsessed with *Downton Abbey.*" *TV Guide*, January 24, 2013.

Tony Rennell, "Downstairs at Downton: How real servants worked 14-hour days." *Daily Mail*, October 15, 2010.

Lucy Wallis, "Servants—The True Story of Life Below Stairs." BBC, September 22, 2015.

Needles' Eyes, Wealth, Learning, and Virtue

HOW DO THOSE WHO CLAIM TO BE CHRISTIANS today reconcile the modern world's quest for material gain with Jesus's severe injunctions against riches? Most notably in verses 10:25-26 of *The Gospel According to Mark*: "But Jesus answereth again, and saith unto them, Children, how hard is it for them that trust in riches to enter into the kingdom of God! It is easier for a camel to go through the eye of a needle, than for a rich man to enter into the kingdom of God" (King James version).

I suspect a representative answer came from a pink-cheeked young business major when I asked that question in a core literature class years ago. Without a second's hesitation, he told me, "Things were different then."

And so they were. According to theologian Sakari Häkkinen, "In the Ancient world poverty was a visible and common phenomenon. According to estimations 9 out of 10 persons lived close to the subsistence level or below it. There was no middle class. The state did not show much concern for the poor." In fact, exploiting the poor was the primary source of income for the fraction at the financial top who made their fortunes as provincial governors, tax collectors, and moneylenders. By condemning the rich abusers, Jesus was, in effect, preaching to the destitute choir.

Leap ahead fifteen centuries when flourishing pro-to-capitalistic commerce in Europe spread the proceeds of trade, and the good life was enjoyed by an expanding middle class. As seen in the meticulous details in paintings by Jan van Eyck, Pieter de Hooch, Rogier van der Weyden, and others, material objects were prized, driving the accumulation of the profits needed to acquire them.

This new emphasis on the things of this world is explained by Harold J. Cook in *Matters of Exchange: Commerce, Medicine, and Science in the Dutch Golden Age*. Ships sailing about the known world made the acquisition and sharing of physical goods a possible goal. Scientists transformed their field by turning their attention to the study of concrete articles. Nonscientists—a larger number—attributed great value to concrete possessions. An expansion in disposable income led to a consumer revolution. A large proportion of this new wealth was spent on literal consumption. Merchants and others with the means were "acquiring well-crafted furniture, linens, antiquities, painting and sculpture, books and manuscripts, strange and lovely items of nature, and other rare and beautiful objects." Cook concludes that "Valued objects had become 'goods' alongside personal virtues. As the historian of art and society Richard Goldthwaite has put it, 'possessions become an objectification of self,' perhaps 'for the first time.'"

But what about Biblical condemnations of riches? In a period when most Europeans took the Bible much more seriously than they do today, the affluent sought a loophole to avoid the threat of Mark 10:25-26. Would accumulations of fine jewels, linens, and spices of the East condemn the owners to forsaking eternal salvation?

The Renaissance theologian, poet, and historian Caspar Barlaeus (1584–1648) proposed an answer by defending commerce as beneficial to virtue and wisdom. His argument is explained by Cook. Before Barlaeus, Dirk Volkertsz Coornhert, in 1580, wrote that wealth and virtue were compatible if the profits were given to charitable causes or even supporting military defense. The critics of this position asked why anyone would seek profits they couldn't keep.

Barlaeus took a different tact, defending self-interest as natural and essential to social interaction, mutually supporting others and ultimately fulfilling God's purpose for each of us. He claimed that great wealth led to great learning and that virtue and magnificence came from the union of learning and worldly activity. Cook summarizes the core of Barlaeus' beliefs: "It was not from doctrine but from the interactions found in buying and selling, and in the search for knowledge that was another aspect of exchange, that modesty, honesty, and natural truths emerged."

While a camel might be stymied by the needle's eye, a Dutch burgher would sail right through. That is, because for Barlaeus, as much as he defends the basis of capitalism, wealth was not an end in itself but rather a means to the betterment of society and humankind. In his more carefully formulated argument, he echoes my pink-cheeked student in justifying the differences of his period's economic circumstances from the time of Jesus.

Today, we appear to be in a throwback to Galilean imbalance, with wealth burgeoning exponentially for the few. Inequality is escalating, the top 0.1% having as much of the bottom 90%. While the 90% don't live in Galilean poverty, the middle class is withering, the working class falling behind, millions resentful at the loss of what they once had and seeing no promise of regaining it. Rather than following Jesus by threatening the rich with the loss of heaven, they—unaware—are closer to Barlaeus in calling for a reallocation of wealth to achieve a better society. Yet, we are a long way from the modesty, honesty, and truth that might result from a search for knowledge.

Sources

Harold J. Cook. *Matters of Exchange: Commerce, Medicine, and Science in the Dutch Golden Age.* Yale University Press, 2007.

Sakari Häkkinen. "Poverty in the first-century Galilee." *HTS Theological Studies,* 2016.

What is College For?

NOT LONG AGO, I RECEIVED a group email sent to the surviving members of my undergraduate college class announcing—boasting—that the class gift from our sixtieth reunion had been the primary contribution for a golf training facility at Rutgers University. A photograph of the plaque honoring our support accompanied the message.

According to a press release celebrating the Class of 1957 Training Center:

> The state-of-the-art, two-room facility features indoor putting space with *Envyscapes* turf and a hitting bay with *Swing Catalyst* technology, allowing student-athletes from both teams to train year-round. "This is a game changer for our student-athletes to be able to train right where they live," said men's head coach Rob Shutte . . . "On behalf of the entire men's golf team, we can't thank the supporters enough who made this facility a reality."

The nature of that class gift and the pride with which it was offered fed into my ongoing ponderings about the purpose of college, a subject much debated at a time of Covid-19, when many campuses have turned to remote teaching, when many colleges worry about survival, when many current students resent and even sue over the high tuition for online learning, and when many graduates and dropouts complain about the lifetime burden of college debt and low-paying jobs.

During the many years I was an idealistic academic faculty member, I would have shaken my head at such a class gift, wondering what golf had to do with a college education. Now I'm not so sure. Was the real reason for sitting in classrooms, passing exams, and writing papers for four years the ability to devote future decades to lingering on the links? Not that my fellow students could even have imagined such a future in our youth.

I realize that my classmates and I—those of us lucky enough to still be alive in our mid-eighties—enjoyed a very different college experience from that of later and current generations. We coveted tweeds and foulards, turned out papers on manual typewriters, made calls from payphones, and rarely owned our own cars, not even expecting to. And at Rutgers College in the mid 1950s, we were all male. Women attended Douglas College a few miles across town, making a welcome presence at Saturday-night fraternity parties, even though they had to be back in their dorms for a midnight curfew.

We also represented a small percentage of high school graduates, among the less than ten percent who completed college at the time. (By 2019, the rate was thirty-five percent.) Many of us came from working class families with little spare income. Fortunately, tuition was low, and some—like me—had scholarships. For a number of my friends, that scholarship and summer and part-time jobs covered all our expenses. We graduated with no debt.

Not only that, but job opportunities were aplenty. It was a peak of the post-war economy with burgeoning management positions and a competition by businesses to fill them with college-educated people, primarily male.

My classmates ended up with very successful careers, the majority who did not become doctors or lawyers retiring after years in upper management of large corporations. The sons of blue-collar fathers gravitated into the upper middle class. They lived—and continue to live—the good life, many with second homes that became the sites of their retirement, in a number of cases just a few steps from a golf course.

Those hours on pristine green lawns, focused on sending a small ball into a tiny hole, then back to the club house for a few drinks, and occasionally a few hours later for an evening meal, explain to me the class eagerness to support the golf training center. My classmates were happy to spread the beneficence of their success and the hope that today's young students will share similar good lives in the future.

And that's been the dream of students in the decades since we were undergraduates—a version of the American dream. The degree a passport to a good job, a large house, a luxury car, travel, and top-of-the-line golf clubs. While our high school classmates who didn't attend college earned less, lived in smaller homes, drove ordinary cars, traveled more locally, and bowled instead of golfed, they still owned those homes and cars, paid their bills, and prepared their children for the aspirations of college.

Then the economy changed. Well-paid manufacturing jobs began to vanish. Workers became commodities in the drive to maximize corporate profits, victims of management decisions that may have been made on a golf course. Rather than an option, college became a necessity. Without a degree, you could kiss your future good-bye. The statistics are well known—the increasing gap in lifetime earning of those with and without college, the lower rates of marriage and higher of divorce, the greater chance of unemployment, the debt, depression, and drug overdoses.

For millions of young people that's what the purpose of college had become, winning in a zero-sum game, all or nothing. But even that no longer holds with unaffordable tuition, accumulated debt, lower salaries, with jobs that were once held by high school graduates—that displaced group dropping even further down on the social and economic scale.

More and more today it's being asked if college is worth it, if instead our society could provide more efficient and effective alternatives to gain skills for well-paid jobs and even long-term careers.

I consider the dilemma from a perspective quite different from that of economists and politicians. My classmates' golf gift led me to think about my life in comparison with theirs, even though we shared a very similar undergraduate experience sitting in the same classrooms. Many of them got better grades—probably because they were smarter. The extent of my difference took several years to occur to me.

In addition to being a non-golfer, I've ended up living a life much unlike that of my classmates, though I started out like them immediately after graduation when I accepted an offer to become an advertising and sales trainee at General Electric in Schenectady, New York. That's where I had my one and only adventure on a golf course, the Edison Club for management employees. With borrowed clubs, I churned divots in the green and whacked balls into the rough.

But it wasn't this humiliation that made me decide within a few months I didn't want a career as a corporate executive. I surprised myself by deciding to do something that had never occurred to me as an undergraduate student. I would apply to graduate schools, unsure of whether any would want me. It turned out to be my good luck to get into one that allowed me to immerse in Modernism while writing fiction, ending up with the degree for a career as an English professor.

My income ended up being far less than that of my successful classmates, but I can't complain. Money isn't all it's cracked up to be. Still, I acknowledge that in comparison to them I'm an oddball, having developed a very different assumption of what college is all about.

Taking an image from *Tristram Shandy*, I was one of a small group of those riding our hobby horse of obsession with books and ideas, cramming new volumes onto overloaded shelves, quoting lines and passages, parsing insights. My faculty colleagues and I labored under the delusion that the world shared our egghead perspectives, that our true mission was to lead our students into sharing our obsessions.

Some of those students may have considered us with a benign amusement, like watching kitten videos. A few may have been momentarily awed during office visits, as in, "Did you read *all* those books?" At fraternity parties, in my day, we sang ribald songs about our professors, affectionately mocking their mannerisms. But we did our assignments without complaint. Now, in this era of grade inflation, a good number of students seethe at faculty they consider unfair in their assignments and grading policies.

Several years ago, I had a recognition when watching episodes of a Showtime documentary series that followed a group of freshmen at the University of Texas–Austin, supposedly the most selective of that state's public institutions. It may be the results of those who edited hours of footage, but this group of eighteen-year-olds talked of nothing but parties and whether "he" or "she" really liked me, moaning over unrequited crushes and dateless Saturday nights. Not once did one say something like, "I really had this great lecture on Jung's collective unconscious."

But it wasn't like that when I was an undergraduate. In addition to the drive of hormones, my contemporaries in their pre-golfing days could discuss a book or debate an idea. I recall sharing notes with a friend taking a political theory course where we read whole books by Plato, Aristotle, Machiavelli, Hobbes, Locke, Rousseau, and a few others. Overall, most of us were aware of what we should know, authors we should have read, ideas we should know about, a bit guilty that we didn't.

Yet as much as I was eager to learn, I was easily distracted, more drawn by hanging out with friends, extracurricular activities, falling in love, falling out of love, going to movies, decorating fraternity floats, reporting for the campus paper, listening to music, playing cards, watching occasional TV.

But maybe that wasn't so terrible. Perhaps the real purpose of college for us, whether we knew it or not, was to enable us to grow up and become adults. More than information gained, fulfilling course requirements taught us focus and discipline. Interacting with a variety of people brought us lifelong friendships and appreciation of others, the ability to get along. These are the attributes that helped my classmates succeed in their professions and earn the luxury of golf.

Defenders of an education in the liberal arts have long emphasized the path to greater critical thinking and problem-solving. That too has been important for their high earning. And I've also noted a generalization I can make about most who have gone to college, even those who sailed through with minimal effort. They possess a fuller sense of systems, how things connect, than many who did not attend. They are better able to cope with the world around them.

The experience of living on campus or in housing near campus, having to manage your young life without relying on parents, served as a crucial step to self-reliant maturity. College was a rite of passage.

It still is for some, or will be again when Covid-19 is behind us. But those some are no longer young people like me, emerging from a blue-collar world. College—the campus experience—costs far too much for offspring of the shrinking middle class, just about impossible for those of the working class. College perpetuates and exacerbates the growing income and social gap so destructive to American society. It's doubtful that I and a large number of my golfing classmates would be able to attend today, certainly not living on campus with minimal part-time jobs, filling their days and nights with socializing and occasional study, preparing for a future of fulfilling careers and the good life. Or ending up as an oddball egghead with book-crammed shelves.

The educational experience of the future is likely to be very different from mine and even from that of recent years. College is likely to play a shrinking role with the emphasis on developing specific occupational skills for the workforce. That has been the tendency of many existing universities, closing down majors in philosophy and history, minimizing literature to focus on basic writing. Who can afford to devote hours to discussing books and ideas when the accumulation of practical abilities is what matters to prepare for the world of work, when employers demand those abilities?

Writing in *Inc*, Parul Gupta, co-founder of Springboard, a provider of online courses, predicts that "Tangible skills will replace credentials, and learning will be lifelong." She predicts a continuation of remote education taught by mentors who are professionals and hiring managers in touch with the demands of the workforce. Instruction will be personalized, and students will learn at their own pace with individualized feedback. "The next-generation of higher education," she proposes, "will be designed to teach the needed 'on the job' skills, as well as provide opportunities for real-world experience."

Oren Cass, executive director of American Compass, an anti-market conservative group, writing in *The New York Times*, argues that much of the $150 billion spent on public subsidies to college students every year is wasted because only a fraction of young people even complete college, many of those needing additional "trade school" to qualify for a job. He calls for half of the $150 billion to be transferred from higher education to "programs that foster employer-trainee relationships."

Even though Gupta and Cass represent particular social and political perspectives, they share some basic assumption with many university administrators seeking long-term survival of their institutions. A future competition may break out between those hoping to preserve their campus environments and those businesses happy to provide skills instruction to remote students from far-flung keyboards.

What I enjoyed during my four undergraduate years is likely to become a luxury. Except for the occasional athletes who bring in sports revenue, the residential college experience will be limited to the already privileged, progeny of parents at home on the soft turf of golf courses, sons and daughters perfecting their inherited swings and putts in a state-of-the-art training facility.

I wonder when our society achieves a point where the affluent are all under par and the rest are relegated to mastering skills for gainful employment, if we won't have lost something indefinably vital. Those completing what may still be called higher education will no longer receive even minimal exposure to the likes of Plato, Aristotle, Locke, Adam Smith, Dickens, Austen, Woolf, Toni Morrison, Confucius, Lao Tzu, Kierkegaard, Keats, Keynes, and Shakespeare.

That lament may be my sentimental throwback to Matthew Arnold's "the best that has been thought and said." Much more troubling for the larger society is the threat of an exacerbated class gap, an educated few manipulating a majority of worker bees, men and women shaped to fill slots determined by those who decide which skills should be the primary subjects of a corporate or university training system. It would be a different sort of throwback, in this case to a version of the assembly line, one without time clocks but workers still relegated to roles as functionaries.

Hard Times: Teaching Facts

> A general State education is a mere contrivance for molding people to be exactly like one another, and the mold in which it casts them is that which pleases the predominant power in the government, whether this be a monarch, a priesthood, an aristocracy, or the majority of the existing generation. — John Stuart Mill (1806–1873)

FOR MANY YEARS AFTER IMMERSION in Victorian novels during grad school, as much as I enjoyed them, I believed the world and the people they depicted were curiosities. I'd figuratively shake my head at their doings and beliefs, as well as their ponderous garb, furnishings, and architecture, happy to be living in a very different time. But that was delusion. Despite flush toilets, electric cars, and iPhones, we are recapitulating much of the political and economic essence of that era.

Take education. I had long assumed that the words Thomas Gradgrind barks to a classroom of children that open Charles Dickens's 1854 novel *Hard Times* revealed the folly of a benighted time. "Now, what I want is Facts," Gradgrind says. "Teach these boys and girls nothing but Facts. Facts alone are wanted in life." The students are admonished to "discard the word Fancy altogether. You have nothing to do with it."

But then I encountered the budget-cutting educational proposals of certain current governors, primarily Republican, and located the source of their thinking in the March 2011 report of the National Governors Association Center for Best Practices titled "Degrees for What Jobs? Raising Expectations for Universities and Colleges in a Global Economy."

The report praises governors and policymakers in "pioneering states [who] have taken the following steps to strengthen universities and colleges as agents of workforce preparation and sources of more opportunity, more growth, and more competitive advantage:

"Set clear expectations for higher education's role in economic development;

"Emphasize rigorous use of labor market data and other sources to define goals and priorities;

"Encourage employers' input in higher education;

"Require public higher education institutions to collect and publicly report impacts; and

"Emphasize performance as an essential factor in funding."

If Thomas Gradgrind were governor of one of those states today, he would have to update his harangue to, "Now, what I want are Data. Teach these students nothing but Labor Market Data."

Such an educational program would turn out graduates to fulfill roles as chips in the circuit boards of economic development. The present equivalent of the discarded "Fancy" would be study of a field in the liberal arts, such as one that encouraged the reading of Victorian novels.

North Carolina Governor Patrick McCrory made his dismissal of liberal arts quite clear when he stated in a

2013 radio interview with former Secretary of Education Bill Bennett, "If you want to take gender studies, that's fine, go to a private school and take it. But I don't want to subsidize that if that's not going to get someone a job."

Although Wisconsin's Governor Scott Walker later recanted—or blamed staff members for misinterpreting him—he has inspired vigorous protests and angry editorials for apparently proposing to slash the University of Wisconsin's budget and, more pointedly, recast its educational purpose by revising the mission statement. According to Alia Wong, writing in *The Atlantic*, "He apparently wanted to strip out its frills (stuff like 'extended training,' 'public service,' improving 'the human condition,' and 'the search for truth') and inject it with a more practical goal: meeting 'the state's workforce needs.'"

The smoking gun is a December 29, 2014 memo from Nathan Schwanz, Walker's Executive Policy & Budget Analyst, which contains the hand-printed word "Attachment" and a photocopy of the university's mission statement radically recast with crossed-out words and phrases:

36.01 Statement of purpose and mission. (1) ~~The legislature finds it in the public interest to provide~~ There is created [added words] a system of higher education which enables students of all ages, backgrounds and levels of income to participate in the search for knowledge and individual development; ~~which stresses undergraduate teaching as its main priority; which offers selected professional graduate and research programs with emphasis on state and national needs;~~ which fosters diversity of educational opportunity; which promotes service to the public; ~~which makes effective and efficient use of human and physical resources; which functions coop-~~

~~eratively with other educational institutions and systems;~~ and which promotes internal coordination and
the wisest possible use of resources.

(2) The mission of the system is to develop human
<u>resources to meet the state's workforce needs [add-
ed words]</u>, to discover and disseminate knowledge,
~~to extend knowledge and its application beyond the
boundaries of its campuses and to serve and stimulate
society by~~ developing in students heightened intellectual, cultural and human sensitivities, scientific, professional and technological expertise and a sense of
purpose.~~Inherent in this broad mission are methods
of instruction, research, extended training and public
service designed to educate people and improve the
human condition. Basic to every purpose of the system
is the search for truth.~~

Giving attention to the human condition and truth
might be considered the equivalents of Gradgrind's Fancy. Though meeting workforce needs is underlined in the
editing, heightened human sensitivities remain, albeit
linked to "a sense of purpose."

The Texas GOP's platform rejects teaching critical
thinking.

This potential, but not adopted—at least not official-
ly—evisceration of higher education in Wisconsin can
be considered a timid step when compared to the Texas
GOP's 2012 platform's rejection of the introduction of
critical thinking in the state's public school curriculum:

> Knowledge-Based Education – We oppose the teaching
> of Higher Order Thinking Skills (HOTS) (values clari-
> fication), critical thinking skills and similar programs
> that are simply a relabeling of Outcome-Based Educa-
> tion (OBE) (mastery learning) which focus on behav-

ior modification and have the purpose of challenging the student's fixed beliefs and undermining parental authority.

Instead the platform supports "a return to the traditional basics of reading, writing, arithmetic, and citizenship with sufficient discipline to ensure learning and quality educational assessment." This plank harkens back to the emphasis on the same basics—with religion substituted for citizenship—in Victorian schools.

In *Hard Times*, Dickens attacks materialistic utilitarianism and its emphasis on rational practicality. As expected in a Dickens novel, Gradgrind ends up distraught and repentant when he discovers how his method—his fixed beliefs and his parental authority—has destroyed his children's lives. He finally admits, "I had proved my—my system to myself, and I have rigidly administered it; and I must bear the responsibility of its failures."

A real-life victim of a utilitarian education was John Stuart Mill. From his earliest years he was isolated from peers and drilled with Greek, Latin, algebra, geometry, and history, eventually having a breakdown at age twenty from the resulting emotional depravation. The poetry of William Wordsworth played an essential role in Mill's revival as the poetry's Romanticism fed Mill's sensitivities and helped lead to the more flexible complexities of his social and political thinking. In short, he had discovered a place for Fancy. I think he would find that concept equivalent to what he calls "feelings":

What made Wordsworth's poems a medicine for my state of mind, was that they expressed, not mere outward beauty, but states of feeling, and of thought coloured by feeling, under the excitement of beauty. They seemed to be the very culture of the feelings, which I was in quest of. In them I seemed to draw from a source of inward joy, of sympathetic and imaginative pleasure, which could be shared in by all human beings; which had no connection with struggle or imperfection, but would be made richer by every improvement in the physical or social condition of mankind. From them I seemed to learn what would be the perennial sources of happiness, when all the greater evils of life shall have been removed. And I felt myself at once better and happier as I came under their influence.

I fear the National Governors Association will prove a tougher case to convince that inward joy matters as much as economic development.

Sources

Charles Dickens, *Hard Times* (1854).

J.S. Mill, Autobiography (1873).

Kevin Kiley, "Another Liberal Arts Critic," *Inside Higher Ed*, January 30, 2013.

National Governors Association Center for Best Practices, *Degrees for What Jobs: Raising Expectations for Universities and Colleges in a Global Economy,* March 23, 2011.

Valerie Strauss, "Texas GOP rejects 'critical thinking' skills. Really." *The Washington Post*, July 9, 2012.

Wisconsin Idea Drafting Notes, Madison.com—copy of December 29, 2014 memo from Nathan Schwanz.

Alia Wong, "The Governor Who (Maybe) Tried to Kill Liberal-Arts Education." *The Atlantic*, February 11, 2015.

Guns, Death, Terrorism, the United States

[This piece was written in response to the 2015 San Bernardino shootings. But the issue is hardy passé. Many subsequent examples reveal that the problem is very much with us.]

Details are still emerging about the San Bernardino shootings, but evidence mounts that this was terrorism. Public reaction appears to be much more disturbed and fearful than it was a few days earlier when a lone domestic gunman shot people at a Colorado Springs Planned Parenthood office. The extent of the San Bernardino reaction is understandable because it reveals once more a network of organized forces hostile to Americans, impersonally seeking victims in a variety of public settings. The danger seems far greater. But evidence from recent years reveals we are much more at risk from ordinary gun violence than terrorism. Note that the San Bernardino terrorists' guns were purchased legally just like those of other shooters. If a terrorist or non-terrorist American wants to shoot people, weapons are abundant and easily acquired.

Various news media outfits keep trying to get Americans to realize what's happening. For example:

In October, Linda Qiu, for *Politifact*, did a "fact-check," comparing data from various sources on U.S.

gun deaths and terrorism deaths for the past decade. She found that the total gun deaths were in the range of 300,000 while the number killed in all extremist attacks had been 71. Extending the number to Americans killed throughout the world over a ten-year period, "From 2004 to 2014, 303 Americans were killed in terrorist attacks worldwide, according to State Department reports. During that same time frame, 320,523 Americans were killed because of gun violence."

It's unlikely that former New Jersey Governor and Presidential hopeful Chris Christie was thinking of the number of three- to six-year-old American children with lethal guns when he pledged to ban Syrian orphans. But *Opposing Views* has reported that, in the first half of 2013, eleven children in that age group killed themselves or a playmate with a gun they thought was a toy. During that same period, domestic terrorists killed four people with homemade explosives at the Boston Marathon.

"U.S. Leads World in Mass Shootings" the *Wall Street Journal* reminded us in October 21015. The article cited Adam Lankford, an associate professor at the University of Alabama Department of Criminal Justice. He found that countries with higher rates of gun ownership recorded more mass shooters per capita. The U.S. ranks first in gun ownership per capita, with roughly 270 million firearms, or 89 firearms per 100 residents. Yemen ranks second, with an estimated 55 firearms per 100 residents.

The U.S. represents less than 5% of the 7.3 billion global population but accounted for 31% of global mass shooters during the period from 1966 to 2012, more than any other country, Mr. Lankford told the *Journal*, noting that the technical definition of a mass-shooter is a person who has killed at least four victims at a go. The 90 killers who carried out mass shootings in the U.S. amount to five times as many as the next highest country, the Philippines. In *Salon*, Heather Digby Parton reminded readers: "Recall that in December of 2001, as Attorney General John Ashcroft was rounding up American and foreign Muslims by the hundreds, he refused to allow the FBI to check records to see if any of them had bought guns."

The *New York Daily News* on November 18, 2015 splashed the headline "NRA'S SICK JIHAD" on its front page, blaming the organization for blocking a bill in Congress that would deny those on the government's no-fly suspected terrorist list the right to buy weapons.

Right on the heels of this came stories about how Texas Representative Tony Dale, who serves on the House Committee on Homeland Security and Public Safety, had sent a letter to his state's Governor and Texas state leaders warning them that Texas laws would allow newly arrived Syrians to arm themselves almost immediately.

San Bernardino is far from an isolated situation. Since the beginning of 2015, there have been at least 354 reported cases of mass shootings. According to shootingtracker.com these took place in about 220 cities in 47 states.

Where Evil Lies: The Transformation of Charles Dickens

WAS JOSEPH CONRAD RIGHT in *Heart of Darkness* in asserting that civil behavior is only a fragile veneer disguising an underlying viciousness? Is such viciousness a lurking ember that just needs some incendiary spark to burst into flames? Or, rather than unleashing a potential festering within them, are the destroyers themselves captives of a subsuming external force?

Charles Dickens, a writer known to many only through "A Christmas Carol," might be assumed the opposite of Conrad and an encompassing evil. Instead, his heartwarming tale associates Dickens with a warm fire, a hearty pudding, a loving family, and—more centrally—the ability of the human heart to reveal its essential goodness. That turns out to be a simplistic grasp of Dickens.

In his novels written over thirty years, from *The Pickwick Papers* and *Oliver Twist* to Bleak House, *Little Dorrit*, and *Our Mutual Friend*, he confronts—perhaps unconsciously—the question of where evil lies, revealing a transformation of attitude that can be seen in the fundamental change between his early and later novels. In effect, the difference dramatizes both sides of the argument between the aberration of an evil exception or an inherently violent human nature, ripe for disorder.

"A Christmas Carol" (1843) was written early in Dickens' career. In the story, Ebenezer Scrooge, a self-ish, miserly, nasty man who has mistreated others and scorned Christmas, breaks down with guilt when a Phantom in a graveyard shows him his own tombstone: "'Spirit!' he cried, tightly clutching at its robe, "hear me! I am not the man I was. I will not be the man I must have been but for this intercourse. Why show me this, if I am past all hope!" He is not, of course. Once admitting his transgressions and begging forgiveness, Scrooge soars in his redemption: "I am as light as a feather, I am as happy as an angel, I am as merry as a schoolboy. I am as giddy as a drunken man. A merry Christmas to everybody! A happy New Year to all the world. Hallo here! Whoop! Hallo!" For the Dickens of this tale, even the worst of men can purify his heart through a sudden conversion. The evil in him is swept away.

"A Christmas Carol" is just a novella. A Dickens novel is usually much longer, hundreds of pages, involving a large cast of characters and an involved plot, often in which a young innocent struggles against villains even worse that Scrooge, villains guilty of physical abuse and criminal activities, even murder. In the value system of the early Dickens, the soft heart is opposed to the hard heart, selfless love to cruel mercenary selfishness. Villains are driven by avariciousness and sexual lust; mothers even sell their daughters; pure love is sullied.

The narrative interest revolves around conflicts of good and evil: threats to the heroine, dangers to the hero, multiplying tensions and mysteries. Dickens, in those early novels, manipulates sets of moral givens. His treatment of evil is simple, wickedness clearly labeled and personified in characters like Squeers of *Nicholas Nickleby* (1839), and Bill Sykes and Fagin of *Oliver Twist* (1839). They are despicable men, lacking any redeeming virtues. But once they are punished or removed, the world rights itself, harmony restored, the innocents free to rejoice in happy lives.

The sum total of evil in these novels results from the negative attributes of the villains. Thus, the evil is clearly explicable and immediately concrete. Such evil exists because men do not follow the true values of an ideal love. All that is wicked and negative in the world has its source in hard-hearted individuals, and if only they would change—like Scrooge—they too would ascend into bliss.

For example, the final chapter of *Oliver Twist* contains a tabulation of what happened to all the characters, the punishments of the guilty and the rewards of the innocent, including the fate of the boy who is the novel's title character:

> Mr. Brownlow adopted Oliver as his son. Removing with him and the old housekeeper to within a mile of the parsonage-house, where his dear friends resided, he gratified the only remaining wish of Oliver's warm and earnest heart, and thus linked together a little society, whose condition approached as nearly to one of perfect happiness as can ever be known in this changing world.

The later Dickens is unable to offer such an easy solution, a world cleansed of villains that rights itself into a state of near perfect happiness.

In the earlier novels, therefore, while a feeling of evil may pervade the atmosphere, it is incarnated in individual characters. After *Bleak House* (1853), this explanation no longer holds. Now the source of evil is not even concrete; it lies beyond any single character or the sum of negative characters. While they still exist, such characters are not the initiators of evil but themselves tools of a malignant force, figures acting out a larger pattern and trapped even more hopelessly than the positive characters.

The character from whom evil emerges, like Compeyson in *Great Expectations* (1861), is a shadowy presence, an indefinite mysterious figure lurking behind the scene, frightening because his nature cannot be defined. And he cannot be defeated or removed from the world that permeates the lives of all the characters. This terror is expressed by Pip, the novel's narrator, when he reveals his reaction to Compeyson:

> I could not have said what I was afraid of, for my fear was altogether undefined and vague, but there was a great fear upon me. As I walked to the hotel, I felt that a dread, even exceeding the mere apprehension of a painful or disagreeable recognition, made me tremble. I am confident that it took no distinction of shape, and that it was the revival for a few minutes of the terror of childhood.

Of all Dickens' passages that capture the trap the envelopes people, the description of fog that opens *Bleak House* is the most vivid. The fog is a form of paralysis; it blurs and blinds; it is everywhere, burying objects in an indistinguishable haze, negating time and movement.

Mud accumulates crust upon crust. One cannot be certain that the day has begun; one imagines the death of the sun.

Evil in the later novels is not just embodied in a collection of villains. It is a force beyond character that cannot be dismissed with the defeat of those villains, who are themselves trapped in an overwhelming and all-encompassing evil. Its center cannot be named or resisted.

In an analysis of *Little Dorrit* (1857), the critic J. H. Miller writes. ". . . evil exceeds any particularization of it, and we are left at the end with an undefined unpurged sense of menace." That novel's ending, despite the marriage of the title character and Arthur Clennam that would have signaled a triumph in early Dickens at this point in his writing career, is far from a purging. The couple have resolved nothing; they merely escape into a passivity: "into a modest life of usefulness and happiness," clinging to each other to avoid being engulfed by a roaring world.

The survival of the virtuous in the later novels is a hollow victory, qualified by the expense of the great suffering that had preceded it and the uncertainly of the future to follow. Good does not win out merely because it is good. More unsettling is the fact that good cannot even comprehend all that it is fighting, the nature of the ultimate enemy.

The trajectory of Dickens' novels can be seen as a loss of innocence, from the triumph of the purified heart to a realm that holds no hope of an escape from an enveloping darkness.

WALTER CUMMINS has published seven short story collections—*Witness, Where We Live, Local Music, The End of the Circle, The Lost Ones, Habitat: stories of bent realism, Telling Stories: Old and New.* He also has published three collections of essays and reviews—*Knowing Writers* and *Death Cancer Madness and Meaning,* and *Irresponsible and Maladjusted.*

More than one hundred of his stories, as well as memoirs, essays, and reviews, have appeared in magazines. With Thomas E. Kennedy, he is founding co-publisher of Serving House Books, an imprint for novels, memoirs, and story, poetry, and essay collections. For more than twenty years, he was editor of *The Literary Review.* He is now editor emeritus.

His other publications include *Our Literary Travels* and *The Literary Traveler,* co-written with Thomas E. Kennedy; *Programming Our Lives: Television and American Identity,* co-written with George Gordon; and collaboration on five books about the Vanderbilt-Twombly Florham Estate in New Jersey.

He is a professor of English Emeritus at the Florham Campus of Fairleigh Dickinson University, where he taught in the MFA Program in Creative Writing and the MA Program in Creative Writing and Literature for Educators. His degrees are a BA in English from Rutgers and an MA in Humanities, MFA in Creative Writing, and PhD in English from the University of Iowa.